American Folk Painting

AMERICAN FOLK PAINTING

by
Mary Black
and
Jean Lipman

BRAMHALL HOUSE
NEW YORK

This 1987 edition is published by Bramhall House, distributed
by Crown Publishers, Inc., 225 Park Avenue South, New York,
New York, 10003, by arrangement with Clarkson N. Potter, Inc.

Printed and Bound in Italy

Library of Congress Cataloging-in-Publication Data

Black, Mary (Mary C.)
American folk painting.

Originally published: New York : C.N. Potter, 1966.
Bibliography: p.
Includes index.
1. Painting, American.   2. Primitivism in art—
United States.   3. Folk art—United States.   I. Lipman,
Jean, 1909-   . II. Title.
ND205.5.P74B59   1987   759.13   87-2971
ISBN 0-517-09732-X

h g f e d c b

INTRODUCTION

Hanging on the dark wall beside the staircase in my grandfather's house were four big portraits of my ancestors; faces, hands, bonnets, and collars gleamed in pale contrast against clothes and backgrounds as dark as the wall. I remember them always, but my awareness of them came slowly. Eventually they became personages more real than some of my bearded great-uncles and their frail wives who lived near us on the outskirts of our New England town.

My grandfather could ring off the names of our common forebears like a practiced litany. "The old man is your great-great-great grandfather, Hosea, and the woman with a shawl is his wife, Elizabeth. The younger man is their son Phillips with his wife, Frances."

He told me more; his stories, along with their strict Yankee visages, made the quartet seem so alive that I alternately longed and feared to mount the stairs past them at night. I was not alone in this. Often my brother and I would watch them from between the stair rails in the upper hall; as we crept along the floor we looked at them. It seemed to us that they looked back, following us with solemn eyes.

Many years later the portraits became mine. As my grandmother and I brought them down from the attic of her family's house, the same feeling of touching friendly ghosts came over me. It seemed to me that for whatever purpose these faces had been created, it had been fulfilled, not only for my great-grandparents, the unknown artist's immediate patrons, but for generations beside that he had not dreamed of serving.

As time went by, I began to see the paintings as something more than startlingly realistic portrayals. When I finally became aware that they were not only faithful likenesses but well-organized compositions that emphasized faces by contrasts and highlighting of costume and gesture, the renaissance of interest in American folk art was well under way.

Appreciation of these paintings as works of art began slowly in the boom years of the twenties, gained momentum in the thirties and forties, and came to fruition in the 1950's with the founding of museums devoted exclusively to folk art. At first the works of nineteenth-century limners were discovered and collected by twentieth-century painters and sculptors who were themselves innovators and experimenters in revolt against traditional forms and techniques. In the strong innocent art of their predecessors these artists found a similar spirit pursued for a different reason; removed from the teaching of academies and professionals, the folk painter found his own solutions to painting problems.

Recognition of the works of the self-taught ranks progressed as museums and art dealers accepted these country productions, and as collectors of modern art in the thirties looked to folk paintings and sculptures as the spiritual ancestors of then current trends.

The enthusiasts who wrote on folk art early in its return to favor found numerous parallels between the work of provincial limners and leading modern artists, comparisons that would certainly have astonished the untutored painters of the eighteenth and nineteenth centuries. However, account books, ledgers, and journals record the economic stability of the folk artist and his general social acceptance by his peers. His paintings are testimony to the artist's practical purpose, a record of faces and the introduction of color and design into houses in the country and in small towns.

It is more than forty years since the first exhibitions of folk art took place in a few museums, historical societies, and art galleries. The Whitney Studio Club of New York City (now the Whitney Museum of American Art) was among the first with its "Early American Art" show of 1924. The exhibition was organized by one of its artist members at the request of its director, Juliana Force. That same year, folk exhibitions were held at New York's Dudensing Gallery and in Kent, Connecticut. In 1927 the Studio Club showed the collection of Isabel Carlton Wilde of Cambridge, Massachusetts, a dealer in folk art who had shown American primitives at her own studio the year before.

The artists who began the revival include Elie Nadelman, who exhibited folk art at his home in Riverdale, New York, as early as 1926; Robert Laurent, Alexander Brook, Yasuo Kuniyoshi, Bernard Karfoil, Stephan Hirsch, Charles Sheeler, and William Zorach. Many of them had loaned examples that they owned to the early show at the Whitney Studio Club.

But it was the first museum exhibitions at Newark in 1930 and 1931, combined and repeated at the Museum of Modern Art in 1932 that marked the real return of folk art to public favor. Holger Cahill became the first writer to deal with American folk art as a subject worthy of scholarly investigation, and the first of many art historians and museum directors and curators to consider folk art as an authentic art expression. He, along with Elinor Robinson and Dorothy Miller, documented the exhibitions at the Whitney, the Newark Museum, and the Museum of Modern Art. Mr. Cahill was not only an innovator in organizing museum showings of folk art, but later became the director of the Index of American Design. The Index, established in 1935 by the Smithsonian Institution, was a visual artists' record of eighteenth- and nineteenth-century American design that gave further impetus to recognition of untutored American artists, as did a WPA artists' project in New England charged with recording the portraits of that region.

As owner of the Downtown Gallery in New York, Edith Gregor Halpert pioneered in collecting, showing, and promoting American folk art. In the fall of 1931 she opened the American Folk Art Gallery and began to sell and exhibit folk art there. Among those whom Mrs. Halpert advised in their new interest was Abby Aldrich Rockefeller, one of the founders of the Museum of Modern Art. Mrs. Rockefeller's was the first important collection that remains intact. In 1935, following the 1932 exhibition at the Museum of Modern Art in which all but two pieces were anonymous loans from her collection, she loaned—and later gave—most of the paintings to Colonial Williamsburg. Since 1957 her augmented collection has been housed in a handsome museum there.

Apart from a number of learned and authoritative catalogues of exhibitions and collections, only four full-length books have been published on American folk painting. The first volume, *American Primitive Painting* by Jean Lipman, was followed six months later by Carl Drepperd's *American Provincial Painting*, in 1942; Alice Ford's *Pictorial Folk Art* was published in 1949, and Mrs. Lipman and Alice Winchester's *Primitive Painters in America* was printed the following year.

Until 1932 folk art exhibitions were most often small and specialized; a bewildering miscellany of manufactured pieces was exhibited alongside the works, good and bad, of untutored painters and carvers. Since the mid-twenties knowledge of the artists and their works has increased enormously along with critical evaluations of their works. Superior examples have made their way into public and private collections devoted exclusively to folk art, and are gradually taking their place in leading art museums with broad collecting interests. Currently, fine examples are on view at the Abby Aldrich Rockefeller Folk Art Collection in Williamsburg, Virginia; the Edgar William and Bernice Chrysler Garbisch collections at the National Gallery in Washington and the Metropolitan Museum in New York; at Fenimore House in Cooperstown, New York; the Webb Gallery at Shelburne Museum, Shelburne, Vermont; the M. and M. Karolik Collection at the Museum of Fine Arts, Boston; Old Sturbridge Village, Sturbridge, Massachusetts; and at the Museum of Early American Folk Art in New York. Besides these, a number of leading museums and historical societies have small collections that they display with pride as notable artistic expressions by American artist-craftsmen.

The purpose of this book is to present the folk artist as he appeared in his time and place and as his work is appraised today. In this the authors have had the advantage of building their knowledge on the scholarly endeavors of the artists, critics, and art historians who are contemporaries or who have preceded them as enthusiastic advocates of American folk painting.

—Mary Black

FOREWORD

In 1942, in my book titled *American Primitive Painting*, my introduction focused on the importance of considering this field as a major chapter in the history of American art; this point no longer needs to be made. But I went a step further, to quote:

"The style of the typical American primitive is at every point based upon an essentially non-optical vision. It is a style depending upon what the artist knew rather than upon what he saw, and so the facts of physical reality were largely sifted through the mind and personality of the painter. The degree of excellence in one of these primitive paintings depends upon the clarity, energy and coherence of the artist's mental picture rather than upon the beauty or interest actually inherent in the subject matter, and upon the artist's instinctive sense of color and design when transposing his mental pictures onto a painted surface rather than upon a technical facility for reconstructing in paint his observations of nature. . . . And radical though this may seem, it is the author's firm belief that a small number of highly gifted primitive painters, unhampered by any external requirements or restrictions, arrived at a power and originality and beauty which was not surpassed by the greatest of the academic American painters."

—JEAN LIPMAN

ACKNOWLEDGMENTS

T HE AUTHORS are indebted to the following individuals and museums. Most of the people and institutions listed have made contributions to this book so great that it would be difficult to express adequate thanks. Those whose help was less have made this project a pleasant one by their cooperation and interest.

Miss Mary Allis, Fairfield, Conn.
Mr. Albert Baragwanath, New York, N. Y.
Mr. Edward Barnsley, Newton, Pa.
Mr. John H. Bereman, Aurora, Ill.
Miss Margaret Bernstein, New York, N. Y.
Mr. George Bird, Dearborn, Mich.
Mrs. Eugene Bond, Dorset, Vt.
Mrs. R. Barlet Bradshaw, Bronxville, N. Y.
Mr. Robert Burgess, Newport News, Va.
Mrs. Holger Cahill, New York, N. Y.
Mr. William Campbell, Washington, D. C.
Mr. Robert Carle, New York, N. Y.
Mr. Robert Carlen, Philadelphia, Pa.
Miss Elizabeth Claire, New York, N. Y.
Mr. George Cole, Albany, N. Y.
Mrs. Wanda Corn, Ossining, N. Y.
Mrs. George Cortelyou, Rumson, N. J.
Mr. William F. Davidson, New York, N. Y.
Miss Agnes Dods, Montague, Mass.
Miss Louisa Dresser, Worcester, Mass.
Mr. Philip H. Dunbar, Hartford, Conn.
Mr. Wilson Duprey, New York, N. Y.
Mr. Sterling Emerson, Shelburne, Vt.
Mr. Bruce Etchison, Williamsburg, Va.
Mr. Stuart Feld, New York, N. Y.
Miss Alice Ford, Washington, D. C.
Mr. William Francis, Richmond, Va.
Mr. Alfred Frankenstein, San Francisco, Calif.
Mr. Reginald French, Amherst, Mass.
Colonel and Mrs. Edgar W. Garbisch, New York, N. Y.
Mr. Albert Ten Eyck Gardner, New York, N. Y.
Mr. Lloyd C. Goodrich, New York, N. Y.
Mr. Stewart Gregory, Wilton, Conn.
Mr. Martin Grossman, New York, N. Y.

Mrs. Edith Gregor Halpert, New York, N. Y.
Mr. Thompson Harlow, Hartford, Conn.
Mr. William H. Harrison, Harvard, Mass.
Mr. and Mrs. Denison Hatch, Riverside, Conn.
Mr. Bartlett Hayes, Jr., Andover, Mass.
Mrs. Carey S. Hayward, Pittsfield, Mass.
Mr. Herbert W. Hemphill, Jr., New York, N. Y.
Miss Cornelia Hicks, Newtown, Pa.
Miss Jean Hildreth, Williamsburg, Va.
Mr. and Mrs. Lawrence Holdridge, Baltimore, Md.
Miss Frances Jones, Princeton, N. J.
Dr. and Mrs. Louis C. Jones, Cooperstown, N. Y.
Dr. Otto Kallir, New York, N. Y.
Mrs. Jacob M. Kaplan, New York, N. Y.
Mr. and Mrs. Sheldon Keck, Cooperstown, N. Y.
Mrs. Chester Kerr, New Haven, Conn.
Mr. Robert Kimball, Pittsfield, Mass.
Mr. and Mrs. Stanley Lee, Newtown, Pa.
Mrs. Bertram K. Little, Brookline, Mass.
Miss Janet R. MacFarlane, Albany, N. Y.
Mr. Joseph B. Martinson, New York, N. Y.
Mr. Thomas Maytham, Boston, Mass.
Miss Ruth Miles, Egremont, Mass.
Mrs. Lawrence K. Miller, Pittsfield, Mass.
Miss Agnes Mongan, Cambridge, Mass.
Mr. Thomas Mumford, Griffin, Ind.
Mr. Harry Shaw Newman, New York, N. Y.
Mr. William Pierson, Williamstown, Mass.
Dr. Dallas Pratt, New York, N. Y.
Mr. Philip Purrington, New Bedford, Mass.
Mr. and Mrs. Russell Quandt, Washington, D. C.
Mr. Perry Rathbone, Boston, Mass.
Miss Frances Raynolds, Cooperstown, N. Y.
Mr. Norman Rice, Albany, N. Y.

Mr. Frederick B. Robinson, Springfield, Mass.
Mr. Clifford W. Schaefer, New York, N. Y.
Dr. and Mrs. Kurt T. Schmidt, Williamsburg, Va.
Mr. Marvin Schwartz, New York, N. Y.
Mrs. Samuel Schwartz, Paterson, N. J.
Miss Carolyn Scoon, New York, N. Y.
Mr. Donald A. Shelley, Dearborn, Mich.
Mr. Arthur Smith, Williamsburg, Va.
Mr. Bradley Smith, Shelburne, Vt.
Mr. Harold Sniffen, Newport News, Va.

Mr. Frank O. Spinney, Cooperstown, N. Y.
Mr. and Mrs. Nathan C. Starr, New York, N. Y.
Mr. Frederick Sweet, Chicago, Ill.
Mr. Thomas Thorne, Williamsburg, Va.
Mr. Frederick Tolles, Swarthmore, Pa.
Mrs. James Turner, Roanoke, Va.
Mr. Robert Turner, York, Pa.
Mr. William L. Warren, Hartford, Conn.
Mr. Mitchell A. Wilder, Fort Worth, Tex.
Miss Alice Winchester, New York, N. Y.

Abby Aldrich Rockefeller Folk Art Collection, Williamsburg, Va.
Adams National Historic Site, Quincy, Mass.
Albany Institute of History and Art, Albany, N. Y.
American Museum in Britain, Bath, England
Art Institute of Chicago, Chicago, Ill.
Art Museum, Princeton University, Princeton, N. J.
British Museum, London, England
Chicago Historical Society, Chicago, Ill.
Connecticut Historical Society, Hartford, Conn.
Encyclopaedia Britannica Collection, New York, N. Y.
Fogg Art Museum, Harvard University, Cambridge, Mass.
Fruitlands Museum, Harvard University, Cambridge, Mass.
Galerie St. Etienne, New York, N. Y.
Gilcrease Institute, Tulsa, Okla.
Hancock Shaker Village, Hancock, Mass.
The Henry Francis du Pont Winterthur Museum, Winterthur, Del.
Historical Society of York County, York, Pa.
Long Island Historical Society, Brooklyn, N. Y.
Lyman Allyn Museum, New London, Conn.
Marblehead Historical Society, Marblehead, Mass.
Mariners Museum, Newport News, Va.
Massachusetts Historical Society, Boston, Mass.
Metropolitan Museum of Art, New York, N .Y.
Moravian Historical Society, Nazareth, Pa.
Munson-Williams-Proctor Institute, Utica, N. Y.
Museum of Art, Rhode Island School of Design, Providence, R. I.
Museum of Early American Folk Art, New York, N. Y.
Museum of Fine Arts, Boston, Mass.
Museum of Fine Arts, Springfield, Mass.
Museum of Modern Art, New York, N. Y.
National Gallery of Art, Washington, D. C.
Newark Museum, Newark, N. J.
New-York Historical Society, New York, N. Y.
New York State Historical Association, Cooperstown, N. Y.
Old Cushman Tavern, Webster Corner, Me.
Old Dartmouth Historical Society and Whaling Museum, New Bedford, Mass.
Old Sturbridge Village, Sturbridge, Mass.
Pennsylvania Academy of the Fine Arts, Philadelphia, Pa.
Philadelphia Museum of Art, Philadelphia, Pa.
The Phillips Collection, Washington, D. C.
Shelburne Museum, Shelburne, Vt.
Smithsonian Institution, Washington, D. C.
Virginia Museum of Fine Arts, Richmond, Va.
Wadsworth Atheneum, Hartford, Conn.
Whitney Museum of American Art, New York, N. Y.
Worcester Art Museum, Worcester, Mass.
Yale University Art Gallery, New Haven, Conn.

CONTENTS

LIST OF ILLUSTRATIONS

American Folk Painting

THE COLONIAL PERIOD

THE TRADITION OF ART that was transplanted here by the first Protestants and gentlemen adventurers bloomed and flourished in the original thirteen colonies and beyond. Romanticism became the guiding philosophy that influenced the American folk artist in his heyday, but in the colonial period earlier generations of painters imitated the English and Dutch models of the late seventeenth and eighteenth centuries. While John White's watercolors, the first paintings associated with the English colonization, were of the country's wonders, people and wild life, these were followed almost entirely by portraits of the colonists. The land around remained but faces changed and vanished and the portrait became a practical record of oneself or one's loved ones. In the three centers of major activity, southeastern New England, New York Hudson River towns as far north as Albany and Tidewater Virginia, two different trends existed side by side and—sometimes—within each portrait. On the one hand, pose, costume and background were transposed more or less directly from English mezzotints in the classical style; to these, boldly realistic faces and typically American details were added. The copper engravings used as sources were notable for their velvety tones of gray through black; the American addition was a fresh, vital palette.

While mezzotints seem to be the models for the handful of Virginia portraits known, certain New England and New York artists began to paint in a manner that flourished until the common use of the camera. Their attention to bright color, flat, unshaded form and surface design and ornamentation turned back to the art of medieval days, to the tradition that was maintained in England to the time of Elizabeth I. As in medieval art, colonial portraits that are not modeled on prints devote equal emphasis to every detail of background, costume and face. It is more than a slavish copying of styles that the artists or their ancestors knew in the countries of their origin.

1.

The lack of emphasis, even lack of organization and composition, followed as a direct result of little training. It proceeded from the artist's desire to show in a single canvas all that he could see before him—even, in some cases, anatomical details, designs, furnishings or architecture that could not be seen from a single, concentrated point of view.

Within fifty years of the founding of the colonies provincial paintings were created in America. Even before, a visitor to North Carolina returned home with the first English impressions of the New World. The works of John White at Roanoke, unlike most colonial paintings, are not only portraits but an accurate and vital record of the living habits, customs, villages, fishing, agriculture and religion of the natives of the New World (Figs. 1, 2).

In the seventeenth century Evert Duyckinck the First in New York and Thomas Child in Boston were craftsmen-painters. Child probably painted the hatchments and devices used as trappings in funeral processions and Duyckinck decorated glass and painted fire buckets. Both may have been portrait limners besides. In his 1740 obituary, Nathaniel Emmons of Boston is mentioned as a landscape painter.

In the South, John White was succeeded more than a hundred and twenty-five years later by another Englishman. Mark Catesby came to "one of the Sweetest Countreys I ever saw" to illustrate in watercolor the birds and plants of the New World. In his only painting, known through a print as well as in the original watercolor, Bishop Roberts of Charleston recorded a detailed image of the waterfront of his town in 1737/38.

Among the earliest colonial faces that survive in paint are the portraits of members of the Freake, Gibbs and Mason families of Boston. All are in the Tudor tradition. The Gibbs and Mason limner (Figs. 3, 4) and the Freake limner (Fig. 5) show accurate portrayals of colonial dress and, one supposes, the faces of the Bay Colony as well.

While it was a sin in the eyes of the church to worship—or even to have —carved images, Massachusetts portraits painted before 1700 bear witness to the fact that both Church and State encouraged the limning of faces. The costumes and the backgrounds shown in these early paintings are in sharp contrast to the traditional picture of Massachusetts residents. The costumes are sometimes somber, unadorned gray or white or black, but as often as not the crossed shawls of the women sport lace borders, fancy shoes peep out beneath their skirts and rich fabrics gleam in their dresses. The floors, on which the figures are set like wooden dolls, are painted in what we seldom think of as Puritan designs.

A dozen paintings from Virginia, all the members of the Brodnax and Jaquelin families, the leading citizens of Jamestown in 1722, are the only productions by an unidentified painter that still exist. The artist followed the eighteenth-century custom of using mezzotints for poses and costumes, and life itself for the distinctive faces. The charming painting of *Elizabeth Brodnax* (Fig. 6) faithfully follows a mezzotint of Princess Anne. Her young neighbor *Edward Jaquelin, Jr.* (Fig. 7) is painted in pose and costume that are repeated in New York State portraiture. An interesting addition to this likeness is the Carolina green parakeet that in the eighteenth century ravaged the fields and darkened the sky as far north as Virginia in the hot summer months.

North to New York, eighteenth-century patroon portraits sometimes show hard-bitten Dutch countenances. But the exceptions are notable. The calm, still beauty of *Mrs. Petrus Vas* is heightened by a flowing white scarf that hoods her head and frames her face (Fig. 8). This portrait is the key painting in attributing a body of work to Pieter Vanderlyn, who was the son-in-law of Mrs. Vas and the grandfather of John Vanderlyn, who identified his ancestor as a portrait painter.

The eighteenth-century portraitists of the Hudson formed the first school of American art although most of the painters are identified only by their styles. Glens, Gansevoorts, Winnes, Wendells, Schuylers and Sanderses of the Albany area sat for their portraits along with other prosperous merchants and their peers. The serene, colorful style of the artist identified as the Gansevoort Limner is illustrated in the portraits of *Magdalena Gansevoort* of about 1729 (Fig. 9), *Adam Winne* of about 1730 (Fig. 10) and *Debra Glen* (Fig. 11) painted at about the time of her marriage to John Sanders in 1739.

The Wendells of Albany employed several artists. Among the most interesting is the painter of the portrait of *Abraham Wendell* (Fig. 12). Wendell's pose and costume are probably copied from a mezzotint, but in the background is a miniature landscape showing the influential patroon's own hill, stream, lands and mill.

About 1768 the remarkably talented artist John Durand, working in New York, painted the colorful group portrait, *The Children of Garret Rapalje* (Fig. 14). Durand was in Connecticut briefly about 1770, and is believed to have painted portraits of two unidentified children posed in a charming garden against a trellised wall (Fig. 13).

While a mezzotint might have been the model for *Ann Pollard*'s long tapering fingers, the face of the hundred-year-old ancient of Boston (Fig. 15) so far transcends any source but life itself that it becomes one of the masterpieces of American art in its exaggerated realism. The archaic style and stiff pose, almost like a carving, are surprisingly similar to the great self-portrait by the twentieth-century folk painter John Kane.

At a period when folk artists began to move from the centers of their earliest activity up the rivers and along the coast to find new patrons, Joseph Badger of Boston became the tie between Scottish John Smibert and native-born John Singleton Copley. Badger's style, in which static figures whose heads seem to end at their foreheads are set against stylized landscapes, is illustrated in *Two Children* (Fig. 16).

In one of the few scenes of daily life that remains from the colonial period (Fig. 17), Moses Marcy takes a cup of punch in a landscape filled with evidences of the easy comfort of his life: land, house, ship, pipe and account book.

The flyer

FIG. 1. JOHN WHITE. *Indian Conjuror*. Watercolor, 1585.
British Museum

Their rype corne
Their greene corne.
Corne newly sprong.
Their sitting at meate
The place of solemne prayer
The howse wherin the Tombe of their Herounds standeth.
SECOTON.
A Ceremony in their prayers with strange iestures and songs dansing abowt posts carued on the topps lyke mens faces.
7

FIG. 2. JOHN WHITE. *Indian Village of Secoton.* Watercolor, 1585.
British Museum

FIG. 3. Artist unknown. *Henry Gibbs.* Oil, about 1670.
Collection of Mrs. David M. Giltinan

FIG. 4. Artist unknown. *Alice Mason*. Oil, 1670.
Adams National Historic Site

FIG. 5. Artist unknown. *Mrs. Elizabeth Freake and Baby Mary.* Oil, about 1674.
Worcester Art Museum

FIG. 6. Artist unknown.
Elizabeth Brodnax. Oil, about 1722.
Collection of William F. Brodnax, III

FIG. 7. Artist unknown.
Edward Jaquelin, Jr. Oil, about 1722.
Virginia Museum of Fine Arts

FIG. 8. Attributed to Pieter Vanderlyn.
Mrs. Petrus Vas. Oil, 1723.
Albany Institute of History and Art

FIG. 9. Artist unknown. *Magdalena Gansevoort.*
Oil, about 1729.
Henry Francis du Pont Winterthur Museum

FIG. 10. Artist unknown. *Adam Winne.*
Oil, about 1730.
Henry Francis du Pont Winterthur Museum

FIG. 11. Artist unknown. *Debra Glen*. Oil, about 1739.
Abby Aldrich Rockefeller Folk Art Collection

FIG. 12. Artist unknown. *Abraham Wendell.* Oil, about 1737.
Albany Institute of History and Art

FIG. 13. JOHN DURAND. *Children in a Garden*. Oil, about 1770.
Connecticut Historical Society

FIG. 14. JOHN DURAND.
The Children of Garret Rapalje.
Oil, about 1768. New-York Historical Society

FIG. 15. Artist unknown. *Ann Pollard*. Oil, 1721.
Massachusetts Historical Society

FIG. 16. JOSEPH BADGER. *Two Children*. Oil, about 1752.
Abby Aldrich Rockefeller Folk Art Collection

FIG. 17. Artist unknown. *Moses Marcy in a Landscape*. Oil, about 1760.
Old Sturbridge Village

BETWEEN TWO WARS—

THE HEYDAY OF THE AMERICAN FOLK ARTIST

For the American folk painter the end of the Revolution marked his own declaration of independence; a period of great prosperity and production began that lasted almost three quarters of a century. Folk art has always been the gift and expression of the middle class for its peers; it flowers best where the middling sort prevail. For this reason, the greatest number of paintings are from the northeastern states, where the middle class was both dominant and sizable. Esthetic expressions by painters who have learned through their own creations continue to the present day—although modern folk art is most often created by old people who have remained in a closed culture for most of their lives, or by simple artisans who extend their crafts to painted illustrations of their work, dreams or environment. But by far the greatest tide of folk art dates to the early years of the new republic when the ordinary man had some time and money for leisure. It ebbs with the common use of the camera.

The work produced by these painters is characterized by static poses and flat, shadowless forms. The folk artist generally has difficulty in expressing roundness whether the subject is an apple or Eve. He has trouble with anatomy and perspective. Faces are often realistic, but in folk painting one rarely sees a nude; even rarer is any sexual connotation.

As often happens in modern painting, a subject and his familiar attributes and surroundings are approached from many angles; in the case of the folk artist the work impresses the contemporary viewer as being more successful than the artist realized. In portraits, precariously angled shoulders, gangling arms and hidden hands frequently lead to fascinating compositions in which attention is directed to the subject's face.

The artists were split into amateur and professional ranks. Many of the latter learned the use and properties of the tools of their profession from artisan techniques. A few had the benefit of observing the work of other trained artists while a few studied briefly with well-known professionals; yet in their own performances, unique solutions to difficult problems led to distinctive styles. Amateurs painted for the fun of it in their leisure time. Schoolgirls and young ladies were taught by schoolmasters or drawing masters to copy and combine sources into compositions that ranged from the mediocre to the marvelous. A Sunday artist, who might be a doctor, storekeeper, housewife or seamstress during the week, took brush in hand to delineate as best he could the likeness of wife, child, house or farm. An itinerant artist took to the road carrying the tools of his craft and traveled from town to town and from house to house. Other professionals worked within their own regions for relatives, friends and neighbors.

The life and scenes the folk artist depicted were images on a small scale rather than on a grand one. Honesty and straightforwardness shine through the faces that peer, warily or innocently, from above ornate costumes and stock poses. These pictures gave farmers and innkeepers and housewives a sense of importance that only a record of their faces and belongings could give—an immortality that served to remind their children of what their fathers had been. Even more important than this view of social history is the fact that many of the provincial artists' paintings have esthetic value of their own: a vitality, simplicity and strength unique in American art.

Their painting method was superior to their draftsmanship. Unlike the work of some modern artists, few of the paintings of these artisan-craftsmen fail because of poorly stretched or prepared canvas, or bad or galling paint. Whatever the failings in plasticity, perspective or anatomy, the folk artist's use of quality materials is consistent, part of the learning-through-doing process that led to individuality of expression.

Working in small towns or traveling in rural areas, the folk artist made a unique record of American life. He gave to country people an art distinctively their own. He performed a necessary and positive function for his patrons, who called upon him to portray themselves and their children, to decorate their walls or to re-create their town, to paint the events of their daily lives and their patriotic and religious beliefs.

The Professional Portrait Painter

FROM THE FOUNDING of the Republic to the eve of the Civil War, the provincial portrait painter flourished in his trade. Itinerant or resident artist, this professional was the chief source of folk paintings that were high in quality and great in quantity. A rare and splendid painter-craftsman like Edward Hicks might find commissions for other subjects than faces, but for most master painters, delineation of honest likenesses enhanced by best clothes and parlors was their chief trade. Schoolmaster, schoolgirl and Sunday painter added romantic and religious emphasis to the vast outpouring of pictures, but it was the portrait painter who filled the essential needs of country art patrons.

Late in the nineteenth century the legend grew that the country portraitist sat by the fire in the winter sketching and painting bodies of men, women and children for his summer travels. Next the itinerant is discovered on the road, his wagon bristling with a variety of frames, stretched and painted canvases and a good supply of paint for filling in the blanks where the faces should be. As he progressed from farm to town, this legendary figure knocked at every door offering, for a small sum, to paint in faces to suit the features of each household.

It is a wonderful story endlessly repeated by grandfathers, novelists and art experts. Its only flaw is that it doesn't seem to be true. The remarkable folk painters of the nineteenth century were more likely than not to keep accounts, write letters and even manage journals of their activities and travels. The headless body is not mentioned. More important, among literally thousands of folk portraits that exist today not one is without a head. The opposite, in fact, is true; not only are there paintings of faces in which the costume is outlined only in a sketch, but in artists' saving ways the reverse of several canvases show sketches of faces and heads above no body at all.

Certainly it is easy to believe, seeing a bright face painted above a dark dress and background that this was the final touch. Perhaps the story took shape late in the nineteenth century from elegant photography parlors where almost everything but the face was furnished. It might have grown in another way. After 1860, former itinerants made large and colorful copies of daguerreotypes and tintypes, sometimes combining them into group portraits. With these mechanics to guide him the artist might begin wherever he pleased: feet, body or head first.

Every folk artist favored certain backgrounds, furniture and props and these came to be as much a part of his style as his personal tricks for creating good likenesses; but family jewels, buttons, furniture, bonnets and laces that still exist—in fact as well as in portraits—give additional support to the professional method of the folk artist at the peak of his career. In this respect he worked as his academically trained brother did. The head was first sketched from life; then costume, prop and background were filled in according to an attractive formula that the folk artist learned early and well.

The professional portrait painter was a fine craftsman as well as a good and diplomatic judge of character. Frequently he ground his own expensive pigments into equally dear oil vehicles. He mounted and stretched his canvases, and often made his own frames. The portrait was sketched in on canvases prepared and sized with ground coats that varied with individual preference or current style. More often than not the paint was applied in thin layers. Finally, one or more glazes of varnish served to stabilize and protect the pigment.

THE PROFESSIONAL PORTRAIT PAINTER, 1780–1810

THIS, ONE OF the great ages of the folk artist in America, is almost exclusively the history of portrait painters from Connecticut. Boston and cities and towns along the Hudson had been the chief centers for folk portraits in the colonial period; the new spate of activity in this line that took the professional to almost every corner of Connecticut—and beyond—was due chiefly to improvement of roads, and the subsequent opening of once-isolated communities. New leisure came with the development of towns and cultivation of lands. While families, even whole villages, had transplanted themselves up the river valleys and along the New England coast in the colonial period, the Republic saw its prospering citizens improving and embellishing the lands and houses in which they and their ancestors had lived. While four years of depression followed the end of the war a new era of prosperity began in the late 1780s in which the portrait painter was encouraged in his trade.

The excitement of independence fairly won is reflected in portraits in which the subjects were the first national members of a rising middle class. The new generation of Connecticut painters, led by Winthrop Chandler, began work just before the Revolution. Chandler was not only the first of the group of artists who were to record the features of residents of the State of Connecticut but he set a tradition in finding his chief patrons among relations and near neighbors that later folk painters followed more or less closely.

Winthrop Chandler was born in Woodstock in 1747. His portraits of *Reverend and Mrs. Ebenezer Devotion,* painted in Scotland, Connecticut, in 1770, when the artist was twenty-three, are his first known and one of his most important commissions. According to a history of Worcester, Massachusetts (where the artist, "poor, and deseased, insolvent," spent his last sad, debt-ridden years), Chandler had studied portrait painting in Boston. He was a decorative painter as well as a limner; the families of numerous Boston craftsmen had Connecticut connections. The friends and acquaintances of these Bostonians included a number of portrait painters whose styles Chandler might have imitated. Yet in the best of his paintings, which include the likenesses of his older brother and his sister-in-law, *Captain Samuel Chandler* and *Mrs. Samuel Chandler* (Figs. 18, 19), there is a lively exuberance quite unlike the painting of anyone in or out of either Boston or Connecticut.

Samuel Chandler fought in the Revolution; it is probable that one of the engagements in which he took part is seen beyond the window. The portrait of Mrs. Chandler is even more boldly delineated than her husband's. Visible artist's changes in chair, drapery and dress have enlarged upon the lively interplay of color, design and pattern. Both figures dominate the canvases; yet every inch of leftover space is spent in describing their lives and circumstances.

Chandler probably inspired another precedent that folk painters were to follow. While the artists who crisscrossed New England and upstate New York were seldom taught by their predecessors, echoes of familiar styles recur in the work of painters who traveled the same territory. In the case of

Chandler two anonymous artists and another, Reuben Moulthrop, seem to have known his work.

One of the unknowns painted the controlled but relaxed likeness of *Oliver Wight* from Sturbridge (Fig. 20), a town just northeast of Woodstock, Massachusetts. The Chandler influence was probably from portraits and not acquaintance, for the painting dates to about 1790, the year Chandler died. In contrast to the romanticism of Wight's portrait is the realistic likeness of *Jonathan Dwight, I* (Fig. 21). But both paintings are unusual in the pale palettes employed by the unknown artists, both using oils in hues most often reserved for pastels or watercolors.

As far as is known, Reuben Moulthrop, born in East Haven, Connecticut, never overlapped in time or place with Winthrop Chandler, yet several portraits attributed to Moulthrop are tantalizing because the style follows Chandler's in several respects. On the basis of similarity to the few signed portraits by Moulthrop, other likenesses are attributed to him. In their abundant attention to detail, *James Reynolds* and his wife, *Mary Kimberly Reynolds* (Figs. 22, 23), are strongly reminiscent of the canvases jammed with books, flowers, drapery and furniture by Chandler. In Moulthrop's paintings, however, the personality of the sitters triumphs persuasively over details.

Moulthrop began his career as a sculptor of wax portrait heads; there is an impression of greater solidity in his figures than in the flat likenesses of most folk painters. Yet hands and clothes have shadowy, dark outlines that are peculiarly Moulthrop's style. Many of his paintings are in poor condition, severely crazed or alligatored through Moulthrop's use of thick paint and an incompatible binding substance. While the Reynolds' portraits are slightly later than the portrait of *John Mix* of New Haven (Fig. 24), dated 1788, the lack of conventional props in the Mix portrait brings it closer to the signed and dated portrait of the *Reverend Ezra Stiles* that Moulthrop painted in 1794. Painted the same year as Ezra Stiles is a charming portrait of two girls. The attractive figures of *Elizabeth and Mary Daggett* fill the canvas; their gestures are as wooden as those of their eighteenth-century doll (Fig. 25).

While Moulthrop continued to paint through the first decade of the nineteenth century, attributions of portraits to him remain controversial because of dramatic changes in style and wide variations in the handling of his subjects—even between companion portraits of husband and wife.

In contrast to the shadowy people of Reuben Moulthrop—softly outlined and stepping forth from dim backgrounds—are six crystal-clear portraits of the Denison family of Stonington, Connecticut, painted by an unknown artist in the early 1790s. The characters of *Captain Elisha Denison* and his wife, *Elizabeth Noyes Denison,* are as sharply etched as the details of their prosperous lives that fill the backgrounds (Figs. 26, 27). Their four children, *Elizabeth* (Fig. 28), *Matilda* (Fig. 29), *Elisha, Jr.* (Fig. 30) and the youngest, *Phebe* (Fig. 31), are beautifully costumed and set in an attractive array of Connecticut interiors and exteriors that almost provide an inventory of Denison holdings.

The unknown painter of the Denisons used a harder and more incisive line than his contemporary Joseph Steward, whose paintings reflect a warm sympathy between sitter and artist. Steward was born just over the Massachusetts line in Upton. Upon graduation from Dartmouth he was licensed as a minister, but illness forced him to abandon this vocation and led him to move to Hartford where he worked as a painter; in 1797 he opened a museum in the State House. Steward's portrait of *Jeremiah Halsey* of about that year shows the State House in the background (Fig. 32). Halsey had not only contributed funds for its completion but had also paid for the chair in which he sits, one of a set of twelve. The angularity of the subject's forearms directs attention to the law library and State House and makes a diamond-shaped composition in which Halsey's face is the apex.

Perhaps the most appealing of Connecticut artists was John Brewster, Jr., a deaf-mute born in Hampton in 1766. Young Brewster not only received instruction from Steward, but probably knew the work of Winthrop Chandler as well, for Chandler painted subjects in Windham County, the boyhood home of Brewster's father. While the gentle influence of Steward is visible in an early portrait of Brewster's father and stepmother, *Dr. and Mrs. John Brewster* (Fig. 33), Brewster's technique—crisp and lively—shows mastery of a style that exceeded Steward's in subtle charm. In 1796, Brewster's younger brother Royal moved to Buxton, Maine, where he took up his father's profession. For John this provided a distant home where he was warmly welcomed. Two lovely, still portraits of a boy and girl, traditionally identified as the son and daughter of a traveling physician, may be the painter's nephew and niece (Figs. 34, 35). Subtle combinations of dark color and pattern emphasize the fair faces of the pair. The boy is set full-length in space against a patterned floor. His pose, costume and the finch he holds on one finger all recall Goya's *Don Manuel Orsorio de Zuñiga,* a subject the country painter could not have known in any form.

Part of the measure of Brewster's courage and acceptance of his infirmity was his enrollment—at the age of fifty-one—in the first school for the deaf in America, established in Hartford in 1817. In twenty years only two students supported themselves at the Asylum for Deaf and Dumb Persons—one was John Brewster, Jr.

One of Brewster's finest works and a landmark in American painting is the calm, beautiful portrait of *Sarah Prince* of Newburyport, Massachusetts, shown seated at a pianoforte and holding a copy of a popular turn-of-the-century composition, "The Silver Moon" (Fig. 36). It is touching to find the artist to whom the world was silent portraying the girl against this background. The color is a warm monochromatic symphony—white shading to cream with tones of brown and black. While there is a stillness and solemnity in the girl's pose and countenance, there is gaiety in the musical notes echoed in the painted bellflower design on the keyboard cover.

For all her youth Sarah Prince dominates Brewster's large canvas, but the most monolithic figures in American folk art were created by Simon Fitch of Lebanon, Connecticut. Fitch may have served in the Revolution; from 1793 to 1799 he was an officer of the Connecticut militia and held the rank of captain in his last years of service, a title that appears frequently in connection with his painting career.

John Trumbull attended the same school as Simon Fitch and lived for a time in the same town, but the work of the two artists contrasts: Trumbull skillfully painted vast and complicated historical pieces, while Fitch, teaching himself by observation and imitation, produced the masterful portraits of *Ephraim Starr* and *Hannah Beach Starr* of Goshen (Figs. 37, 38). Painted in 1802, they are his best work. Ephraim Starr is set on a patterned floor—the design of which may be a pun on the sitter's name—and is seen as though the artist sat slightly above his subject; by this device the solid bulk of Starr's figure makes it seem ready to burst from the canvas. Mrs. Starr is more placid; in her iridescent gown she looks immovable as she gazes slightly downward at the painter. Her one wandering eye—which the painter specifies—is part of the realism blended with romanticism that was to become more pronounced as the century progressed.

A painter who emphasized a realistic approach was William Jennys, a figure who appears mysteriously about 1790 working in the manner and style of a relative, Richard Jennys. William, after traveling all the New England states except Rhode Island and Maine, disappears before 1805 as mysteriously as he came. But there is little mystery concerning the faces and personalities of the sturdy Yankees whom he portrayed. *Hannah French Bacon* (Fig. 39) is shown in a splendid cap, collar and taffeta gown with a ribbon belt pinned with the subject's own buckle, which is still preserved. The signed portrait, dated 1795, is a vision of a clear-featured and attractive young matron. While Jennys often assayed fine clothes and jewels, he avoided as often as possible the problem of showing hands. The splendidly dressed young dandy identified as *Nathaniel Lamson* of Stratford, Connecticut (Fig. 40), shows his hand tucked into his waistcoat. The boy has a slightly haughty glance. He is one of the few subjects by Jennys whose likeness is not enclosed within a painted oval spandrel.

The familiar oval may once have surrounded a cut-down portrait of an unknown *Woman with Long Blonde Hair* painted about 1800 (Fig. 41). The painting is almost a caricature, but like other Jennys' subjects the figure is solid and occupies volume in space in direct contrast to the flatness characteristic of most folk artists.

While Jennys' whereabouts in New England are known for only fifteen years, the influence of his style is seen in the later works of Reuben Moulthrop and Simon Fitch (though Fitch courageously attempts the whole figure, generally with some style). Jennys may also have influenced Nathaniel Wales, who probably traveled from Litchfield, Connecticut, to Oswego, New York, to paint the likeness of a former Middletown, Connecticut, resident, *Mrs. Nathan Sage* (Fig. 42). The Sages lived in Oswego in 1806, the date of the portrait.

In western Massachusetts, still another painter was influenced by Connecticut painting and by the work of Jennys in particular. Nothing is known of the artist beyond his name, J. Brown, and the fact that he was in Cheshire,

Massachusetts, in 1808 when he signed and dated the portraits of *Mercy Barnes Hall* (Fig. 43); her husband, the innkeeper *Calvin Hall* (Fig. 44), and their daughter, *Laura Hall* (Fig. 45). It is an extraordinary trio. Their flinty, wary-eyed features contrast sharply with the elegance of poses and costumes. Unlike Jennys, J. Brown did not fret over problems of anatomy, and Laura is shown full-length—from Medusa locks to starred slippers.

In 1810 Brown seems to have moved eastward across the state to Upton (Joseph Steward's birthplace) where he is credited with painting the sweet-faced likeness of *Clarissa Partridge Childs* (Fig. 46). It is the only other portrait assigned to J. Brown, an attribution based on the similarity of technique and style to the Halls. Mrs. Childs's likeness echoes Jennys even more than the Halls.

A few miles east of Upton in Duxbury, Massachusetts, another folk artist was at work. Dr. Rufus Hathaway consistently painted in an archaic style that suggests earlier dates than the ones inscribed, or that the facts of his subjects' lives permit. Extravagantly gowned and hatted, *Mrs. Ezra Weston, Jr.,* daughter-in-law of the town's most prominent citizen, sat for her portrait (Fig. 47). The colors are somber except for her pale face, a contrast that emphasizes the subject's strong features. Even more highly stylized —almost like the carving on a New England headstone—is the chiseled likeness of an unidentified *Lady with Pets*, painted about 1790 (Fig. 48). Here, Hathaway uses contrasting color and design; the paint is alligatored so extensively it almost seems translated to an intricate mosaic pattern.

Contrary to Trumbull's characterization of his home state, Connecticut became a veritable Athens to the self-taught painters of the new republic. While both Jennys and Moulthrop strayed across the borders of Massachusetts and Connecticut to New York State, only a handful of paintings in the early states are equivalent to the glories created by Connecticut's folk artists.

One strict, stylized exception is the portrait of *Reverend Samuel Buell*, a portrait study in black and white of a Long Island clergyman (Fig. 49). Another is *The Colden Family* (Fig. 50) with its dazzling content and strong composition. Colden, son of the royal lieutentant-governor of the Colony, was a Tory and the builder of Coldenham, near Newburgh. Colden, his richly gowned and bejeweled wife, and two of their many grandchildren were portrayed by an unknown artist about 1795. Mrs. Colden grasps the arm of the younger of the two button-eyed children who holds a bird; it seems less eager to escape than its small master. A warm background outlines the solid figures and costumes of the quartet, while an enormous black patch draws attention to Mrs. Colden's plain face.

FIG. 18. **WINTHROP CHANDLER.** *Captain Samuel Chandler.* Oil, about 1780.
National Gallery of Art,
collection of Edgar William and Bernice Chrysler Garbisch

FIG. 19. WINTHROP CHANDLER. *Mrs. Samuel Chandler.* Oil, about 1780.
National Gallery of Art,
collection of Edgar William and Bernice Chrysler Garbisch

FIG. 20. Artist unknown. *Oliver Wight*. Oil, about 1790.
Abby Aldrich Rockefeller Folk Art Collection

FIG. 21. Artist unknown. *Jonathan Dwight, I*. Oil, about 1790.
Metropolitan Museum of Art

FIG. 22. Attributed to Reuben Moulthrop. *Mary Kimberly Reynolds.* Oil, about 1790.
Collection of Nina Fletcher Little

FIG. 23. Attributed to Reuben Moulthrop. *James Reynolds.* Oil, about 1790.
Collection of Nina Fletcher Little

FIG. 24. Attributed to Reuben Moulthrop. *John Mix*. Oil, 1788.
Abby Aldrich Rockefeller Folk Art Collection

FIG. 25. Attributed to Reuben Moulthrop. *Elizabeth and Mary Daggett.*

Oil, about 1794.
Collection of Mary Allis

FIG. 26. Artist unknown.
Captain Elisha Denison.
Oil, about 1792.

FIG. 28. Artist unknown.
Elizabeth Denison, Lady with Plumed Headdress.
Oil, about 1792.

FIG. 27. Artist unknown.
Elizabeth Noyes Denison.
Oil, about 1792.

Collection of Edgar William and Bernice Chrysler Garbisch

FIG. 29. Artist unknown. *Matilda Denison*. Oil, about 1792.
Collection of descendants of Matilda Denison

FIG. 30. Artist unknown. *Elisha Denison, Jr.* Oil, about 1792.
Collection of descendants of Matilda Denison

FIG. 31. Artist unknown. *Phebe Denison*. Oil, about 1792.
National Gallery of Art, collection of Edgar William and Bernice Chrysler Garbisch

FIG. 32. JOSEPH STEWARD. *Jeremiah Halsey*. Oil, about 1797.
Connecticut Historical Society

FIG. 33. JOHN BREWSTER, JR. *Dr. and Mrs. John Brewster.* Oil, about 1790.
Old Sturbridge Village

FIG. 34. JOHN BREWSTER, JR. *Boy with Finch*. Oil, about 1880.
Abby Aldrich Rockefeller Folk Art Collection

FIG. 35. JOHN BREWSTER, JR. *Girl in Green*. Oil, about 1800.
Abby Aldrich Rockefeller Folk Art Collection

FIG. 36. JOHN BREWSTER, JR. *Sarah Prince*. Oil, about 1801.
Collection of Mr. and Mrs. Jacob Kaplan

FIG. 37. SIMON FITCH.
Hannah Beach Starr. Oil, 1802.
Wadsworth Atheneum

FIG. 38. SIMON FITCH.
Ephraim Starr. Oil, 1802.
Wadsworth Atheneum

FIG. 39. WILLIAM JENNYS. *Hannah French Bacon.* Oil, 1795.
Abby Aldrich Rockefeller Folk Art Collection

42.

FIG. 40. WILLIAM JENNYS.
Nathaniel Lamson. Oil, about 1795.
Collection of Mary Allis

FIG. 41. WILLIAM JENNYS.
Woman with Long Blonde Hair.
Oil, about 1800.
Abby Aldrich Rockefeller Folk Art Collection

FIG. 42. NATHANIEL WALES. *Mrs. Nathan Sage.* Oil, 1806.
Collection of Stewart Gregory

FIG. 43. J. BROWN. *Mercy Barnes Hall*. Oil, 1808.
Abby Aldrich Rockefeller Folk Art Collection

FIG. 44. J. BROWN. *Calvin Hall*. Oil, 1808.
Abby Aldrich Rockefeller Folk Art Collection

FIG. 45. J. BROWN. *Laura Hall.* Oil, 1808.
New York State Historical Association

FIG. 46. Attributed to J. Brown. *Clarissa Partridge Childs.* Oil, about 1810.
Abby Aldrich Rockefeller Folk Art Collection

FIG. 47. RUFUS HATHAWAY. *Mrs. Ezra Weston, Jr.* Oil, about 1793.
Collection of Mary Allis

FIG. 48. RUFUS HATHAWAY. *Lady with Pets.* Oil, about 1790.
Metropolitan Museum of Art, collection of Edgar William and Bernice Chrysler Garbisch

FIG. 49. Artist unknown.
Reverend Samuel Buell. Oil, about 1790.
Long Island Historical Society

FIG. 50. Artist unknown. *The Colden Family*. Oil, about 1795.
Abby Aldrich Rockefeller Folk Art Collection

THE PROFESSIONAL PORTRAIT PAINTER, 1810–1840

AT THE END of the Revolution the inland and upland areas of New England, New York and Pennsylvania were beginning to be developed by new settlers. The trend continued for a generation; by the third census in 1810 the country's population was almost two-and-a-half times the total estimated at the end of the war. With the opening of towns and the improvement of transportation, the heyday of the folk artist in America began in earnest. While the preceding decades had produced many painters who knew and sometimes imitated one another's styles, most of the new generation approached paintting as a highly individual expression.

The War of 1812, "Mr. Madison's War" in New England and New York, seemed to accelerate the rising cult of the common man. In small communities where every man was—in some dimension—a king, it was his right to have his likeness taken. Even more, it was a practical necessity for preserving the look of oneself and one's family for future generations.

In Philadelphia, William Street and Jacob Eichholtz began a painted record of the faces of fashionable Pennsylvanians. In the farm country north and west of the city another kind of record was being kept. Unlike most professional folk artists, Jacob Maentel used watercolor exclusively for his full-length portraits of Pennsylvania-German farmers, their wives and children. Despite their small size and Maentel's posing of subjects in stylized profile, the watercolors appear to represent careful and accurate likenesses of his subjects. This artist's pleasure was not only to illustrate his patrons' faces but their brightly costumed figures as well, most of them set against Pennsylvania landscapes or house interiors. Maentel's style is as distinctive as his signature or the printed records he places in his subjects' hands or below several of the full-length figures. A few of Maentel's portraits are earlier than 1810, but the majority of profiles date from that year to the mid-1820s. About 1826, Maentel began to paint his subjects in full-face, a practice that he followed for the remainder of his career; but his portraits in profile are far more interesting and attractive. In *Boy with Rooster* the boy's shock of hair is amusingly reversed and emphasized in the crisp outlining of the rooster's tail (Fig. 51). In contradiction to the facts of life, Maentel endowed his rural subjects with tiny feet and narrow bodies so that the costumes and profiles might be dominant against diminutive pastoral landscapes.

Maentel's *Girl with Fan* is a graceful and charming portrait rather than an exact likeness (Fig. 52). In spite of a rigid pose, face, fan, rose and arms combine to make a harmonious and lively composition. Painted about 1814, the portraits of *Joseph Gardner and His Son, Tempest Tucker Gardner* show tidy Pennsylvania trees and hills dominated by the striding man and his small son (Fig. 53). Maentel's greens often fade to blue, but touches of rich color and sharp delineation of figures and landscape are as crisp today as when first painted.

At about the same time that Maentel began his career, an unknown Pennsylvania artist created the appealing portrait, *Baby in Red Chair* (Fig. 54). In the small canvas the child is a solid and dominant figure fast asleep in a red-painted chair.

In New England, just as the second generation of republican painters set to work, one of America's least known folk artists and one of her best, Ammi Phillips, was beginning his long career; chronicled by dated portraits in a unique style, it spanned fifty years. Although today more than two hundred of Phillips' portraits have been identified, the body of his work is immensely varied, consistent only in a characteristic technique visible in his first known portrait as in his last.

Still, despite signatures and dates in an easily recognizable hand on the reverse of several portraits, inscriptions on gravestones, notices of debts, records of births and marriages, deeds and wills, the personality of the artist remains shadowy, sublimated, one imagines, to the dictates of his profession. He never went far from his home of the moment to find patrons. No portrait in the lot can be securely tied to any town beyond a tight rectangle, fifty miles east and west of the Massachusetts, Connecticut and New York borders; the rectangle was two hundred miles long, with Hoosick and Peekskill, New York, as its most northern and southern boundaries. Phillips' paintings, despite their romantic overtones, are accurate likenesses. Personal style reveals itself in overlarge hands endlessly repeated in set poses; in smooth, careful, fine delineation of faces and hair; in a fondness for the delicacy of muslin and lace; and in characteristic and awkward poses of shoulders and arms. These eccentricities, nevertheless, give rhythm and unity to the spare and economical portraits.

There are numerous hints that suggest Phillips' precarious financial condition. By two wives, Laura Brockway and Jane Ann Calkins, he had ten children. Even if he found painting as profitable an enterprise as other artists, he obviously had difficulty in providing a living for his large family.

Phillips' style underwent numerous changes. *Chloe Allis Judson,* signed by him and dated 1811, is his earliest known work, completed when he was twenty-three. It is a halting, amateur effort; there is only a hint of the great style that immediately succeeds it from about 1813 to 1818, his best period. There is no signed portrait between 1811 and 1820, but serving almost as well are inscriptions and dates in a familiar hand on the reverse of three portraits. The subjects are residents in and near towns where Phillips is known to have lived.

The technique that ties the styles together is already apparent. From whom did it come? Did Phillips, like other folk artists, learn from constant repetition of character, pose, costume and prop? His early period is marked by a surprisingly sophisticated palette—soft, warm pastels with bright flashes of color in dress, accessories and furniture. But the poses of New York border subjects, particularly those of *Harriet Leavens* of Troy (Fig. 55), *Joseph Slade* of Hoosick (Fig. 56), and *Robert Lottridge Dorr* of Chatham (Fig. 57) parrot those of J. Brown. Phillips' portrait of *Harriet Leavens* painted about eight years later than Brown's 1808 portraits of Cheshire, Massachusetts, residents, seems an imitation of the youngest of the Cheshire trio, *Laura Hall.*

A fourth portrait, credited to J. Brown on technical evidence, is of a subject painted in Upton, Massachusetts, about 1810. Upton is three-quarters of the way east in the path from the Berkshires to Boston. If the attribution is correct and the date reasonably accurate, J. Brown had left western Massachusetts at about the same time that Phillips' career began.

Late in the nineteenth century, Phillips is mentioned in a town history as a portrait painter in the 1820s at Pine Plains, New York. His 1820 style is a new one; gone are the hard accurate likenesses and the light palette. In their stead are greater solidity in faces and figures and dark backgrounds against which faces, hands, embroidery and linen stand out with great clarity. *Mrs. Garret Dubois* illustrates the change (Fig. 58). It is strongly reminiscent of Ezra Ames, the Albany artist who in 1820 was at the height of his busy career. That year, his home was only a few miles from Phillips' in Troy. Ames's account and expense books are extensive and his letters numerous, but nowhere is there any reference to Ammi Phillips. Yet, as in the case of J. Brown, portraits by Ames were to be seen nearby. Perhaps the abrupt change in Phillips' style is a chamelon coloration to suit local taste.

In the following decade, Phillips began to develop a mature and distinctive method. Delicate and romantic, his Connecticut portraits of the mid-1830s center on the town of Kent, about twenty-five miles southwest of his birthplace in Colebrook. The winsome charm of this period's subjects is shown in *Woman with an Organdy Collar* (Fig. 59).

In this decade another artist captured a number of patrons in the eastern half of Phillips' empire—Erastus Salisbury Field, born seventeen years after Phillips. In the 1830s Field painted all the members of the Fyler family of Winsted, Connecticut, one of whom was to marry Jane Kinney, Phillips' second cousin and his subject in 1848. Field's robust and static figures are in bold contrast to the delicacy of painting that Phillips employed.

Erastus Field and his twin Salome, named for their parents, were born in May, 1805, in Leverett, Massachusetts. Leverett is a small hill town on the first rise east of the fertile Connecticut Valley. In the second decade of the nineteenth century, New York was three days off, Boston two, and only a few of Leverett's inhabitants had been to either city. In his whole life, Field, one of the most intrepid of Leverett's sons, never went more than two hundred miles from home.

He must have enjoyed all the common work and pleasures of a New England childhood. To these, however, he added a growing ease in sketching portraits of his relatives. His parents encouraged him and provided him with paints with which he experimented on scraps of cardboard. With these, he learned the range and limits of his mediums and skills.

In 1824, the young man took the momentous step of traveling to New York to study with Samuel F. B. Morse. For the first time Morse was enjoying some success in his vocation and was established in a studio at 96 Broadway. He wrote, "My storms are partly over, and a clear and pleasant day is dawning upon me." Just before Christmas in 1824 he conjured up a warmly sympathetic picture of his daily life:

> I have everything very comfortable at my rooms. My two pupils, Mr. Agate and Mr. Field, are very tractable and very useful. I have everything "in Pimlico," as mother would say. . . . I have begun . . . a system of neatness in my painting room which I never could have with Henry. Everything has its place, and every morning the room is swept and all things put in order.

In February, 1825, Morse's beloved young wife died suddenly in New Haven; the tragedy ended Field's instruction. He probably returned to Leverett in the spring, for the portrait of his grandmother *Elizabeth Virtue Ashley*—the earliest of his known works—dates to about that time (Fig. 60). It is a big, powerful composition with broad, smooth planes of color. The old woman's deep-sunk eyes stare wisely toward eternity in this, her last year. A clear, bright accent to the somber palette is the red chair in which she sits.

In 1826, Field took to the road to pursue a profitable career as an itinerant artist. His travels took him across Massachusetts, Connecticut and eastern New York, and lasted for more than a decade. All the portraits of this period show Field's unmistakable and characteristic inability to make figures look real: waists are too short, shoulders too narrow, arms too long. But there is naïve dash, color and style in each. Red chairs with arms ending in curlicues like brown snail shells appear frequently. In Leverett in 1830, Field's younger brother Phineas came of age. In one of his best portrayals, Field marked the event with a fine, sure painting (Fig. 61). The odd proportions—and the red chair—remain. Phineas' nose is broken, his full-lipped mouth pouts, his coarse, straight hair is painted as a design in black folds. The color and line are sophisticated and surprisingly modern.

On a Thursday afternoon, December 29, 1831, Field married Phebe Gilmur of Ware, Massachusetts. The young people lived briefly in Hartford where Field had prospered before, but their first and only child was born in Monson, twelve miles south of Ware, on November 6, 1832. With a wife and baby to support, Field must have felt that he had to work harder than ever, but this must have been a happy and prosperous time for him. His brief study with Morse was a more worldly experience, but he was applying now—on home ground—the lessons learned there. He was experimenting on his own with new and varied effects. Several striking portraits of children date to about 1833. *Ellen Tuttle Bangs* (Fig. 62) and other, younger subjects stand full-length on similar, boldly patterned carpets. Field's expressive shorthand style is readily apparent. The backgrounds range from light to dark neutral tones in billowy cloud effects. All the children have elfin ears and their faces are shaded and highlighted in pointillist applications of gray and pink. Lace and embroidered-muslin patterns are rendered in designs of black dots.

Field's usual method was extremely competent, although occasionally hasty; the canvas was sturdy, the method workmanlike, and even the quick details in expressive painter's shorthand were done with good use of quality materials. He apparently stretched his own canvases, priming them with a base coat of warm light gray.

By late 1836, Field had arrived at his best and most individual portrait style, one that he used until about 1840. From the time he returned to Leverett at Christmas in 1836, the work he produced shows control and mastery of oil portraiture; the draftsmanship is crisp and the painting fresh and incisive. Accurate delineation of character had always been part of Field's method and this continued.

In February, 1838, Field was paid $29 by his cousin Ashley Hubbard for eleven portraits. The Hubbards received full value for their money, for the portraits—all but one of them known—are handsome examples of Field's best style. Sometime before May of that same year, Field painted Jeremiah and Dorcas Gallond and their daughter and son-in-law, Louisa and Nathaniel Cook, in Petersham, Massachusetts. Louisa Gallond Cook, mother of two small children, was fragile and wan; Field portrayed her in the last months of her life.

In the spring, Field, once again in Leverett, painted the winsome portrait of his niece *Ellen Virtue Field* (Fig. 63). Filling the canvas, it is a full-length likeness of the child outdoors with the Massachusetts hills in the background.

Field's commissions for four paintings of the Gallond family led to more work in 1839. Clarissa Gallond was married to William Cook, whose brother Nathaniel had been wed to her sister Louisa. In 1839, Field posed Clarissa at a window overlooking a river landscape (Fig. 64). She had spent most of her life in Petersham and nearby Phillipston, and there is no city on a river in Massachusetts that conforms to the one that Field illustrated. If Field may be credited with artistic license, the river city might be interpreted as Hartford, although the three-masted vessels shown could never have navigated that far. Clarissa is a firm-featured, provincial Portia. She wears a dark dress with a sizable gold buckle at the waistline and one of the largest and most splendid of the embroidered and bowed muslin collars that Field loved to paint. The neckline is secured with a gold and coral pin; her smooth hair is held in place with a saw-toothed tortoise-shell comb set high on her head.

Phebe Field's parents were David and Mary Moore Gilmur of Ware; in 1839 the Field family returned to the Gilmur home on Pleasant Street. Across the street in a comfortable frame house lived Joseph Moore from Windham, Maine, his wife, two children and two orphans. Moore's wife was Almira Gallond, sister of Louisa and Clarissa, daughter of the Gallonds of Petersham. The orphans were Louisa's children. In the Moore's parlor, Field painted one of the landmarks of nineteenth-century American art (Fig. 65)—the Moores and the Cook children appear in a gorgeous array of figures and costumes. Gentler-faced and smaller-featured, Mrs. Moore strongly resembles her sister Clarissa, and wears precisely the same comb, collar, gown, pin and belt buckle. Although no family connection between the Moores of Windham and those of Ware has been established, Joseph Moore's coming to Mary Moore Gilmur's home town seems to indicate that there was a relationship between the two families. *The Family of Joseph Moore* shows Field at the peak of his career as a portrait painter.

Broad mass and clean, spare line characterized the work of many folk painters. About 1835, in the years of the folk artist's greatest prosperity, an unknown artist whose work was almost a blend of Phillips' and Field's style painted *Woman of Sturbridge* (Fig. 66). Delicacy and strength are combined in the young woman's form and face; she is set against an imposing background. The same fine qualities are evident in the fresh and lively portrait of *Mrs. Eunice Spafford* of Holley, New York, by Noah North (Fig. 67). The strong face contrasts with the delicate graining and stenciling of the fancy chair in which she sits.

While the professional portrait painter most often worked with oil on canvas, a few employed pastel or watercolor with equal effectiveness. Micah Williams, an artist whose identified subjects were almost all New Jersey residents, favored pastel. Despite the fragility of the medium there is strength in the facial structure and in the broad masses that define his subjects. *Woman with a Book* (Fig. 68) shows the strong horizontal base Williams established in his portraits of women by posing them with crossed forearms. Fine lacy collars, jewels and curls are decorative accents. The stylized curtain and pillar in this portrait are unusual elegancies for Williams. Similar in pose and period to *Woman with a Book,* but far more stylized, is a watercolor portrait of about the same period by Emily Eastman of Loudon, New Hampshire (Fig. 69). It is one of several graceful portraits by the same artist, all copied from prints.

In dealing with men subjects, Micah Williams achieved unusual strength, even though the medium was pastel. *John Vanderveer* of Freehold, New Jersey (Fig. 70), was portrayed by Williams in 1819 with fine depth of color and robust form.

An unidentified Connecticut artist, working in watercolor, painted *Robert Mitchel* in 1822 (Fig. 71). The strong design of the portrait is reminiscent of fractur. The young man is shown full-length; his features are delicate in contrast to the dark outlines of his square body. He is set against a landscape in which exotic flowering shrubs bloom at either margin of the paper to create a balanced composition.

Watercolor is again the medium in the stark and realistic portrait of *Barnard Stratton* of Amherst, New Hampshire (Fig. 72). Although the painting bears the name of the artist and is dated 1822, it appears to be an inscription done by the sitter or one of his relatives, for a blank is left between the words "Mr." and "Willson" for the artist's first name. It is one of a number of watercolors in the same style, all of New Hampshire subjects. Costume, hair and facial contours are neatly and accurately drawn, giving the impression of a hand accustomed to outlining quick likenesses.

Though the subject has less character than *Barnard Stratton*, the brisk designing and vivid patterning that enliven the watercolor portrait of *Delia Varney* (Fig. 73) mark it as a typical work by Joseph H. Davis. The profiled figure wears a patterned apron and bertha, stands on a patterned carpet and is set against a wall embellished with huge freehand designs. The many colors and designs seem to whirl around the placidly smiling subject to form an exciting background.

The handling of materials and the technique of most self-taught painters show experience in the preparation of support and medium. An occasional artist betrays his lack of competence in portraits that are dramatic but in which draftsmanship and painting are careless and slapdash. Asahel Powers, born in Springfield, Vermont, is just such a painter. His compositions, however, demonstrate to a high degree the folk artist's free and daring way of combining many perspectives in a single painting. *Charles Mortimer French* sits in a country chair (Fig. 74). At his elbow, a squeak box with a toy pug on top is set on a table tipped sidewise for a clear view; a hand-lettered booklet, *My Mother, A Pretty Gift,* floats against the wall on a ribbon hung from a nail. While a variety of textures and woods are accurately suggested, the lines, shadows and highlights etched on the child's face and hands to indicate form give him, instead, the appearance of a small and haggard old man.

In contrast to the rural mannerisms of Powers' art is the elegance of I. Bradley's composition, *The Cellist* (Fig. 75). The full-length seated figure is sensitively set in space, surrounded by music and musical instruments. The painting is clearly signed and is dated 1832; in all likelihood the artist is John Bradley, who worked in New York City in the thirties.

One of the most delightful of all children's portraits is *James Francis Smith* painted by Isaac Sheffield in 1837 when the boy, according to the detailed inscription on the canvas, was five years and ten months old (Fig. 76). James Francis Smith stands on the shore near New London, where the artist lived, a whaling ship shown in the background. It may be the *Chelsea,* the ship belonging to the boy's father. The child wears an extraordinary jacket: "The dress he wore from a voyage in the Ship-Chelsea-from the South Seas-island of desolation." It was made from penguin skins, testifying to the far-ranging voyages of American whalers.

57.

In the portrait of an unknown *Whaling Captain* (Fig. 77), the handsome subject is posed before a conventional red drapery. But the vignette in the background is extraordinary. A whaleboat is dragged by a harpooned whale on a "Nantucket sleigh ride." Aboard the whaler, strips of blubber are cut and hoisted aboard to be rendered in vats on the deck of the ship.

Another interesting background surrounds the portrait of Eliza Smith, Providence schoolmistress (Fig. 78). A church and school drift in the landscape. They are appropriate, for the artist is identified as the pastor of the Broad Street Christian Church in Johnson, Rhode Island. Small, neat Miss Smith sits in a low rocker in a small, tidy floral-carpeted box intended, one imagines, as the abstraction of a room. It is a delightfully imaginative indoor-outdoor setting for an otherwise no-nonsense portrait of a prim schoolteacher.

FIG. 51.   JACOB MAENTEL. *Boy with Rooster*. Watercolor and ink, about 1815.
Henry Francis du Pont Winterthur Museum

FIG. 52. JACOB MAENTEL. *Girl with Fan*. Watercolor and ink, about 1815.
Collection of Martin Grossman

FIG. 53. JACOB MAENTEL. *Joseph Gardner and His Son,
Tempest Tucker Gardner*. Watercolor and ink, about 1814.
Abby Aldrich Rockefeller Folk Art Collection

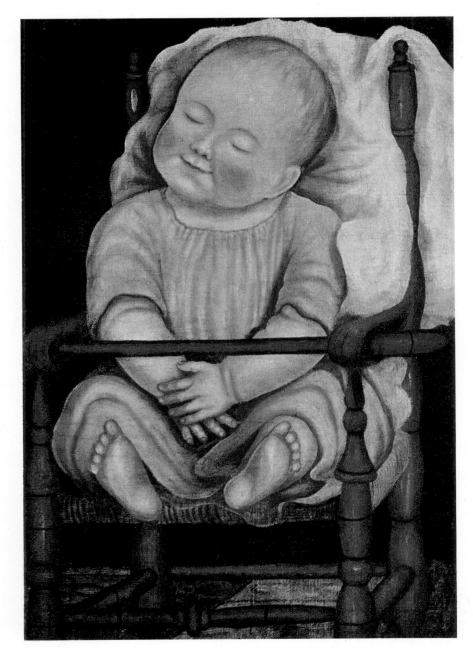

FIG. 54. Artist unknown. *Baby in Red Chair*. Oil, about 1810.
Abby Aldrich Rockefeller Folk Art Collection

FIG. 55. AMMI PHILLIPS. *Harriet Leavens*. Oil, about 1816.
Fogg Art Museum, Harvard University

FIG. 56. AMMI PHILLIPS. *Joseph Slade*. Oil, 1816.
National Gallery of Art, collection of Edgar William and Bernice Chrysler Garbisch

FIG. 57. AMMI PHILLIPS. *Robert Lottridge Dorr*. Oil, about 1814.
Abby Aldrich Rockefeller Folk Art Collection

FIG. 58. AMMI PHILLIPS. *Mrs. Garret Dubois*. Oil, about 1820.
American Museum in Britain

FIG. 59. AMMI PHILLIPS. *Woman with an Organdy Collar.* Oil, about 1835.
Collection of Stewart Gregory

FIG. 60. ERASTUS SALISBURY FIELD.
Elizabeth Virtue Ashley Field. Oil, about 1825.
Museum of Fine Arts, Springfield, Massachusetts

FIG. 61. ERASTUS SALISBURY FIELD. *Phineas Field.* Oil, about 1830.
Collection of Mrs. Carey Stillman Hayward

FIG. 62. ERASTUS SALISBURY FIELD.
Ellen Tuttle Bangs. Oil, about 1833.
Metropolitan Museum of Art, collection of
Edgar William and Bernice Chrysler Garbisch

FIG. 63. ERASTUS SALISBURY FIELD.
Ellen Virtue Field. Oil, about 1838.
Collection of Mrs. Carey Stillman Hayward

FIG. 64. ERASTUS SALISBURY FIELD. *Clarrissa Gallond Cook*. Oil, about 1839.
Shelburne Museum

FIG. 65. ERASTUS SALISBURY FIELD. *The Family of Joseph Moore*. Oil, about 1839.
Museum of Fine Arts, Boston, M. and M. Karolik Collection

FIG. 66. Artist unknown. *Woman of Sturbridge*. Oil, about 1835.
Fruitlands Museum

FIG. 67. NOAH NORTH. *Eunice Spafford.* Oil on wood, 1834.
Shelburne Museum

FIG. 68. MICAH WILLIAMS.
Woman with a Book.
Pastel, about 1820.
Museum of Fine Arts, Boston,
M. and M. Karolik Collection

FIG. 69. EMILY EASTMAN.
Woman with Flowered Veil.
Watercolor, about 1820.
Museum of Fine Arts, Boston,
M. and M. Karolik Collection

FIG. 70. MICAH WILLIAMS. *John Vanderveer*. Pastel, 1819.
Abby Aldrich Rockefeller Folk Art Collection

FIG. 71.   Artist unknown. *Robert Mitchel.* Watercolor, 1822.
Collection of Alfred E. Hamill

FIG. 72. Mr. WILLSON.
Barnard Stratton. Watercolor, 1822.
New York State Historical Association

FIG. 73. JOSEPH H. DAVIS.
Delia Varney. Watercolor, 1837.
Museum of Fine Arts, Boston,
M. and M. Karolik Collection

FIG. 74. **ASAHEL POWERS.** *Charles Mortimer French.* Oil on wood panel, 1839.
New York State Historical Association

FIG. 75. I. BRADLEY. *The Cellist*. Oil, 1832.
Phillips Collection

FIG. 76. ISAAC SHEFFIELD. *James Francis Smith*. Oil, 1837.
Lyman Allyn Museum

FIG. 77.   ISAAC SHEFFIELD. *Whaling Captain*. Oil on wood panel, c. 1835.
Museum of Early American Folk Art

FIG. 78. Artist unknown. *Eliza Smith*. Oil, 1832.
New York State Historical Association

THE PROFESSIONAL PORTRAIT PAINTER, 1840–1850

IN 1837, the painter turned inventor, Samuel F. B. Morse, returned from Paris bringing with him Daguerre's invention. With Dr. John Draper, Morse made the first daguerreotype in America. It is ironic that Morse, a talented artist himself, should have introduced the mechanical device in this country, for the cheap, accurate photograph marked the end of prosperity for portrait painters.

One of the first to suffer was Erastus Field, whose brief study had been with Morse. Field's long painting career extended beyond the third and into the fourth generation of folk painters in the United States. Early in the 1840s Field left Massachusetts for New York City. There he learned the art of photography. On his return to Massachusetts late in the decade he set up a photography studio in Palmer, practicing Morse's plan, "to accumulate for my studio, models for my canvases."

Before his subjects were diminished from imposing, individualistic figures to their new role in society—ordinary people in an expanding world—Field did a few final life-size portraits of friends and relatives. Field's in-laws, the Gilmurs of Ware, were eager to share in his New York adventure and joined him there by twos and threes. The office and residence of David Gilman [sic] "optician," and Erastus S. Field "artist," are listed at 151 Hammond Street in 1845. "Gilman" was probably Phebe Field's older brother. The New York directory for that winter reveals that the small square house close to Pier 54 had other occupants: "Mrs. H. P. Gillmur" and "M. Gillmur." Both sent exhibits to the annual fair in the city, the American Institute of the City of New York. Thousands of exhibits were shown each year, and Samuel Morse's "Electro-Magnetic Telegraph" was an entry in 1842. In 1845, two of Field's relatives sent his paintings to The Fair: Phebe sent an India-ink sketch and M. Gilmur an oil painting. The full-length portrait by Field of a young girl in blue—with costume, furnishings and a warm brown background dating to the 1840s—is identified as *Miss Margaret Gilmore* of Ware, Massachusetts (Fig. 79). It hardly seems that M. Gilmur's Fair entry in 1845 could be any painting but this.

83.

In some places the portrait painter, either through the inaccessibility of his situation or the cheapness of his wares, could hold out for a time against the invading camera. William Matthew Prior and his in-laws, brothers of his wife, Rosamund Hamblen Prior, set up a paint factory, first in Boston and then at Prior's house in East Boston. In their "Painting Garret," the Hamblens and Prior could turn out highly academic portraits, but "Persons wishing for a flat picture can have a likeness without shade or shadow at one quarter price." In several instances the flat likenesses on academy board have prices marked on the back in pencil; one is priced at two dollars and seventeen cents.

The paintings of the relatives by marriage are almost indistinguishable from one another. When the portraits are signed the most placid and least individual figures are more often by Prior than Sturtevant Hamblen, the brother-in-law whose name appears almost as frequently. *Children with Toys* (Fig. 80) and *Man with Gold Pencil* (Fig. 81) are typical examples of the flat, unshadowed portraits that came from the "Garret." Prior and the Hamblens demonstrated that folk painters still maintained an edge over the photographer in their ability to produce large-scale pictures in bright colors; painters could romanticize and stylize their subjects far beyond the nineteenth-century camera's harsh honesty. In *Man with Gold Pencil* the swelling curves of the dark jacket lead the viewer straight to the young man's bright face, a device that the camera could scarcely imitate.

In 1841, a native Vermont painter, Horace Bundy, completed the best of his known portraits, an unidentified *Vermont Lawyer* (Fig. 82). Legal briefs, court orders, law books and a billowy, striped drapery recall details of Winthrop Chandler's portraits of more than sixty years before. In Massachusetts, William Prior was a strong supporter and advocate of the theories of William Miller who prophesied the end of the world and Christ's second coming in 1843, and again in 1844. Bundy was also a Millerite and became a preacher in the Adventist Church. The church was established in 1845 by Miller's followers, who remained faithful to their leader despite his somewhat faulty celestial calculations.

One of the most attractive subjects ever to sit to a folk artist was the young woman identified as *Mrs. Seth Wilkinson* (Fig. 83); according to tradition, her husband was a member of the New York Fire Brigade. About 1845 she was painted by an artist identified only by a familiar style. The unknown artist posed his subjects before an elaborately draped and swagged curtain on a sofa with wooden arms ending in carved roses. His subjects' lace, linen and jewelry are invariably painted in heavy impasto and frame faces that are realistic and well-modeled. The rich surroundings that the unknown artist brought to his patrons created compositions that were the height of middle-class mid-century elegance.

In contrast to Mrs. Wilkinson is the portrait of another New York woman, *Mrs. Jacob Conklin* (Fig. 84). She is as strict and plain as Mrs. Wilkinson is pretty and fashionable. The stark, broad planes of the painting, enlivened only with a blooming rose that dangles from a painted arch, are static. The quiet pose is disrupted only by Mrs. Conklin's tense hands.

A charming watercolor, *Girl in Sprigged Calico* (Fig. 85), captures a child's winsomeness in a realistic way that could not be equaled in a long camera exposure. In contrast, an Illinois couple, *Mr. and Mrs. William Vaughan* (Fig. 86), are portrayed in rigid poses against a background that looks like an early photography studio. The artist, Sheldon Peck of Lombard, Illinois, gave the stern-faced couple small hands and feet, and a great curtain as a backdrop. Amusingly, he painted the end grain of the floor boards, almost as though the couple were seated on a miniature stage; the frame, painted to imitate veneer, forms a proscenium arch above the curtain.

On a small scale, but equally dramatic, are the miniatures of James Sanford Ellsworth (Fig. 87). Ellsworth was born in Connecticut but worked as an itinerant who not only traveled in New England, but ventured as far as Ohio, and perhaps beyond, in search of patrons. In a great many of Ellsworth's portraits, stylized cloud forms are painted behind each head so that profiled features stand out. His subjects are often seated in colorful upholstered Victorian chairs that seem almost to curl around each of the figures.

Painters who were able to maintain successful careers at mid-century continued the tradition of most professional folk artists. Romanticized likenesses, unique stylistic devices and singing color—and cheap prices—made it possible for some to continue even in competition with the camera's all-seeing eye.

FIG. 79. **ERASTUS SALISBURY FIELD.** *Miss Margaret Gilmore.* Oil, about 1845.
Museum of Fine Arts, Boston, gift of Maxim Karolik

FIG. 80. PRIOR-HAMBLEN SCHOOL. *Children with Toys.* Oil, about 1846.
Abby Aldrich Rockefeller Folk Art Collection

FIG. 81. PRIOR-HAMBLEN SCHOOL. *Man with Gold Pencil*. Oil, about 1850.
Collection of Herbert W. Hemphill, Jr.

FIG. 82. HORACE BUNDY. *Vermont Lawyer*. Oil, 1841.
National Gallery of Art, collection of Edgar William and Bernice Chrysler Garbisch

FIG. 83. Artist unknown. *Mrs. Seth Wilkinson*. Oil, about 1845.
Abby Aldrich Rockefeller Folk Art Collection

FIG. 84. Artist unknown. *Mrs. Jacob Conklin*. Oil, about 1845.
National Gallery of Art, collection of Edgar William and Bernice Chrysler Garbisch

FIG. 85.   Artist unknown. *Girl in Sprigged Calico.* Watercolor, about 1850.
Art Museum, Princeton University, Balken Collection

FIG. 86. SHELDON PECK. *Mr. and Mrs. William Vaughan*. Oil, about 1845.
Collection of John H. Bereman

FIG. 87. JAMES SANFORD ELLSWORTH. *Mr. and Mrs. C. T. Gunn.*
Watercolor, about 1845.
Collection of Joseph B. Martinson

Daily Life in the Republic

UNLIKE THE COLONIAL PAINTER whose chief production was the portrait, middle-class citizens of the new states created landscapes and genre scenes by the thousands. Every aspect of American life was illustrated: town and country scenes, house interiors, mourning paintings, parties, games and sporting events. All were precious records of an exciting age. The painters were schoolgirls, housewives, carriage painters, sailors, lumberjacks and professional artists.

More than any other examples of American folk art, paintings of daily life represent not only the esthetic endeavors of the rising middle class but show, besides, homely details that might otherwise be lost. Paintings of real places and events record the architecture, ships, toys, religion and books of the people who ventured to create a new and independent nation.

Even the country artist was sure of his ability to describe what he saw, a certainty not shared by the acerbic Mrs. Trollope who wrote:

> A doubt as to the excellence of their artists is very nervously received, and one gentleman, with much civility, told me, that at the present era, all the world were aware that competition was pretty well at an end between our two nations, and that a little envy might naturally be expected to mix with the surprise with which the mother country beheld the distance at which her colonies were leaving her behind them . . . there is a very considerable degree of natural talent for painting in America, but it has to make its way through darkness and thick night.

GENRE SCENES

THE RUGGED LANDSCAPE was praised by travelers to America who wrote about the beauty of the new country on their return home. But to the settler or to his sons who had won it by war, possession, grant or purchase and then tamed its wild splendors, nothing seemed so beautiful as acres under cultivation. They sought to preserve the vision of pastures and fields, cattle and poultry—and their own portraits in miniature as the uncommon common men who had effected the great change.

Bucks County was a series of low hills and shallow valleys; it rewarded its farmers handsomely in orchards, grain fields and grasslands that yielded rich crops. Livestock came from fine English or American strains and flourished on the fertile land.

No painter captured the abundance of these farms and the inherent beauty of eastern Pennsylvania with greater skill than Edward Hicks. The soft golden light, pink-tinged skies and hazy distances are remarkable and accurate records of the prosperous fields of his neighbors. Serenity fills the air, in contrast to the excitement of the uneasy truces between the ideal and the real worlds in his *Peaceable Kingdoms*. Orphaned as a child, Hicks was apprenticed to a carriage maker when he was only thirteen. From carriage painting he progressed to signs. In 1801 when he was twenty-one, he turned from a life that had been easy and undisciplined to become a Quaker and eventually a Quaker preacher. Hicks's life is well documented by his letters, poems, journals, sermons and diaries, by the houses in which he lived, by books and possessions owned by his descendants, but most of all by his paintings.

Two magnificent farmscapes were painted in October, 1848, and May, 1849, in his last year. *Cornell Farm* (Fig. 88) is "An Indian Summer View," and shows the prize-winning domestic creatures of James Cornell lined up in a horizontal band that fills the lower part of the painting.

In *Leedom Farm* (Fig. 89), his Indian summer mood of the previous autumn is replaced by one of joyous new birth as the artist inscribes his last Bucks County scene, "A May Morning view of the Farm and Stock of DAVID LEEDOM of Newtown Bucks County Pennsylvania with a representation of Himself. Wife. Father. Mother. Brothers. Sisters and nephew." In all the farmscapes the mood is one of remembrance. In the Leedom and Cornell farms the dreamlike middle distance and luminous skies change the farms into fantasies.

Less dreamlike, but no less beautiful are four versions of Hicks's childhood home, *The Residence of David Twining, 1787* (Fig. 90), which Hicks painted from his adult recollection of the farm as it appeared when he first went to live with the Twinings as an orphaned child of three.

The ewe and suckling lamb familiar from the *Kingdoms* and from *Birthplace of William Penn* appear in both *Twining* and *Leedom Farms*. A hired hand plowing behind a team of horses is shown in all the farms but Leedom's where the team and plow remain but not the hired man. Mary Twining Leedom and her husband are set in poses borrowed directly from the engraving that inspired Hicks's paintings of *Washington Crossing the Delaware;* the pair are portrayed again standing in the picture of their son's farm.

Twining Farm is incisive painting; but instead of a unified composition on a single theme, there is a clear staccato beat which draws the eye from scene to scene. The mare and foal and cow and calf at left background are vignettes inspired by newspaper or almanac reproductions of John Anderson's woodcuts; the animals at either side, a well with a sweep handle and an apple press for cider are typical Bucks County fixtures.

The homely details of everyday life among Pennsylvanians in nearby York County were recorded in the opening decades of the nineteenth century by Lewis Miller, a carpenter who drew and colored sketches of the scenes around him as an avocation (Fig. 91). The drawings are, for the most part, illustrations in a series of diaries and notebooks. On one page, a doctor and his family eat their dinner of cornmeal mush amid lively family uproar. Local taverns and the brew house provide backgrounds for other active scenes that accurately describe the life of the county.

Old Plantation (Fig. 92) is a primitive watercolor in which realism dominates; it is one of the few examples of southern folk art in this medium. The fusion of African and southern culture is captured in this document of plantation life. In the background is a view of the main house with its dependencies. In the foreground are boldly accented and individualized figures. While the dress of the slaves is American, the musical instruments, turbans, scarves and stick ceremony attest to the survival of African custom on southern ground. The movement of the three central figures is extraordinary in folk art where static poses prevail. The scene may be the representation of a slave wedding, a ceremony performed in some cultures by jumping over a stick.

The New York State countryside of the 1830s is reflected in a large round canvas by Terence J. Kennedy of Auburn (Fig. 93). The painting records the country's progress; riches of field and stream are guarded by an oversized eagle. A side-wheeler and sailing ship make their way in rough water and are neatly balanced by a canal on the right. Further signs of industry—anvil, plow and bobbin—are shown in the foreground.

A. Dickson Entering Bristol in 1819 (Fig. 94) is rich in associations with the life and times of its subject. Unlike Hicks's *Twining Farm,* the equestrian figure dominates the composition and is the center of interest. Though obviously an important member of his community, nothing is known concerning Dickson, or in fact, the artist, Alexandr Boudro(u), who painted the view more than thirty years later in 1851. Yellow sunlight surrounds the figure that anchors a landscape that threatens to float away in the background. In the nineteenth century, a Bristol Township Inn was located in a community now part of Philadelphia. The surreal quality of this painting on a wood panel is heightened by miniature buildings and blacksmith tools in the foreground, cut down in size so that A. Dickson remains of chief interest.

Even a prison could provide an untutored artist with inspiration. Eunice Griswold Pinney may have been the first American to use this subject, portraying Newgate, a copper mine converted to a jail near her home. Later in the century an unknown artist used a rule and pencil to outline the perspective of the Massachusetts prison at Charlestown (Fig. 95). The prisoners are in rows as neat as the bricks and cell windows. The whole is colored in light, bright watercolor.

A freer view than Charlestown's jail is the world of *Darkytown* (Fig. 96), a reverse painting on glass. Figures are set off in space singly and in pairs as if they are sprightly and individualized participants in a dream.

A similar relation of figures in space may be seen in the foreground of the oil painting, *Market Square, Charleston* (Fig. 97), which is dated to the late 1860s by the presence of a Federal officer at lower right. Street vendors and strolling figures enliven the square dominated by the architecture of Market Hall.

Eunice Pinney was born February 9, 1770, in Simsbury, a small town on the Farmington River in north central Connecticut. She was the fifth of a large family of eight children. Her parents, Elisha and Eunice Viets Griswold, were prosperous and important citizens.

Eunice Pinney's mother taught her children at home during their early years; they developed "habits of persevering industry." The second of the Griswold children, Alexander, who became the first and only Episcopal bishop of the Eastern States Diocese, wrote that he "could read fluently at three years of age." As the children reached their fifth birthdays they were given small farm chores to do. They were taught to knit as well, and the future bishop made "bone-lace" as a child of five.

Eunice Pinney's uncle, her mother's brother, was Roger Viets, the clergyman of the Simsbury parish church; he lived with the Griswold family for several years. During the Revolution he had been imprisoned for his Loyalist sympathies for four months at the Simsbury prison, a location that his niece later recorded in paint. It seems likely that the Griswold family also sympathized with the British cause.

In spite of strict discipline the children had time for amusements, and the bishop recorded his fondness for Shakespeare; he recalled that "The acting of plays was then an occasional chosen amusement with the children of the neighborhood." These diversions appear in his sister's watercolors.

Late in the eighteenth century, Eunice Griswold married Oliver Holcombe of nearby Granby, but before her twenty-seventh birthday she was a widow and mother of two children; Holcombe, bound from Connecticut to Ohio, had drowned fording a stream. In 1797 she married Butler Pinney of Windsor. By him she had three more children. Although Butler Pinney was a native of Windsor, he and his wife moved to Simsbury sometime before 1844 and Eunice is believed to have died in her home town in 1849.

From about 1810 until after 1825 Eunice Pinney devoted part of her time to a wide variety of subjects in watercolor. Her talent was developed through her own study of technique, not through art lessons. Her letters to her daughter, an art teacher in Virginia, contain not only homely advice (some of it in verse), but finished watercolors on the reverse of the written pages for Emeline Minerva to use as models for her students.

Eunice Pinney's style is distinctive. While the faces are expressionless and quickly drawn with economy of line and stroke, her pencil sketches show tidy draftsmanship and careful organization. Her figures are two-dimensional with form subordinated to composition and bold pattern. In her several mourning pictures, faces are often hidden with large and artfully draped handkerchiefs—one suspects a device for getting around the troublesome job of painting features. As is often the case in self-taught artists' work, problems in creating realistic form are apparent.

Figures are elegantly dressed, arrayed in late eighteenth-century style. Long thin arms end in small, stylized hands that are often out of proportion to the figures. But difficulties with features, anatomy and perspective are overshadowed by fresh vigorous color, unusual and wide-ranging subjects and artful composition. Mrs. Pinney's style has mature elegance combined with naïve, and often strangely unrelated design elements.

A curious combination of incidents appears in *Couple and Casualty* (Fig. 98); on the left a rider in Napoleonic soldier's uniform is thrown from his mount and is vaulted over a fence while an amorous soldier and girl in long-armed embrace stand unaffected at the right. The exact composition for the casualty appears in an English copperplate design on cotton. Rounded forms, drawn in two different scales, appear in other Pinney compositions and suggest that the patterns of prized English toiles were used again as inspiration. The source for *The Cotter's Saturday Night* (Fig. 99), in pastel shades against a soft gray background, is almost certainly based on an English aquatint illustrating Burns's poem.

The vigor of Mrs. Pinney's work has been compared to that of the English artist Thomas Rowlandson; while no direct borrowing of Rowlandson's known subjects has been found, the self-taught artist's penchant for modeling from the best source at hand is apparent in many of Eunice Pinney's works. Both *Two Women* (Fig. 100) and *Children Playing* (Fig. 101) are close in idea and form to woodcuts in eighteenth-century children's books.

In *Two Women,* an interior setting with two rigid seated figures, the women appear arrested in space against a background designed to heighten the dramatic effect of each detail. It is one of Mrs. Pinney's finest watercolors. A lighted candle is set on a stand between the women in front of two windows framed by a swagged curtain. The total effect is that of a stage set for a drama that seems imminent.

In an undedicated memorial three large figures are set on either side of a tomb (Fig. 102). A child holds willow branches in its gathered pinafore and clutches the gloved hand of one of the mourners. A small, elongated adult figure—half the size of the other three—mourns, too. Perspective is inversely diminished so that the chief mourner is seen most prominently. The faces of the other full-scale figures are obscured with familiar frilly handkerchiefs.

The child in a pinafore appears again, this time carrying a sheaf of wheat, in the portrait of *Mrs. Clarke the York Magnet* (Fig. 103). Mrs. Clarke, in an empire gown, lounges against an empire day bed. The painting is initialed, signed and dated. A separate black-painted paper is pasted in the background, making a wall behind Mrs. Clarke. A tiny scene, probably a picture cut from an engraving of an interior, is pasted to the black paper.

99.

As a woman of the eighteenth and nineteenth centuries, Eunice Pinney's avocation as a folk artist was unusual. She developed her talents, not with the halting, tentative strokes of the schoolgirl, but with the sure vigor of a mature woman, illustrating for her family and her neighbors her own wide-ranging esthetic and literary interests.

The death of Washington in 1799 led to national mourning. His death and those of relatives and friends were marked by folk paintings in which the graves of the deceased held center stage with the chief mourners. Weeping willows and a church were frequently part of the scene.

One of the most naïve and beautiful of mourning pictures is the watercolor dedicated to Philo Day, with a smaller gravestone marking the grave of Julia Ann Gilbert (Fig. 104). An English drawing book was probably the source for the composition, for there are several other—simpler—versions of the same scene. In this case the unknown artist has added an American touch in the Federal door with fan and side lights.

A mourning picture for *Polly Botsford and Her Children* is an extraordinary composition in which bold, stylized forms are used to create a small masterpiece that presages aspects of modern painting (Fig. 105). The church is reduced to the elements of its framework so that both its interior and exterior appearance are suggested in its triangular skeleton—the idea rather than the actuality of a church. The pointed arches are repeated in the form of the figures, cypresses and fence as well as in the branches and leaves of the large and small willow. A fascinating perspective rapidly diminishing from left to right foreground emphasizes the tombs and mourning figures.

A primitive *Memorial to Daniel Ma . . .* , who died just two years after Washington, shows a complete townscape and an impressive brick town house in addition to the usual elements (Fig. 106). Instead of the black glass mat that surrounds most of these watercolors the margins are embellished with leafy branches and angels.

At mid-century, the highly conventional form of the mourning picture was abandoned. A realistic reminder of the imminence of death in the nineteenth century is given in a view of *York Springs Graveyard* by R. Fibich (Fig. 107), a bucolic country scene with cattle grazing in a pasture adjoining graves enclosed by fences.

The lively, attractive and comfortable homes of the nineteenth-century middle class are portrayed in fascinating paintings that reveal not only individual tastes and preferences but a universal desire for enrichment of furniture, walls and floors.

Canvas floorcloths or wood flooring were stenciled or scored in joyous patterns and colors to imitate expensive carpeting. Walls were hung with bright papers. In the best rooms—dining room, sitting room or parlor—stenciled or freehand designs were painted directly on plaster walls that were most often white. The gayest color of the stencil was usually selected for woodwork.

A clear demonstration that the ordinary middle-class family had family portraits and pretty pieces to ornament its walls is the portrait of Albany's jailer, *Nathan Hawley,* posed with his family in a delightfully descriptive watercolor by William Wilkie in the fall of 1801 (Fig. 108). No less than eight children are shown; all but Mrs. Hawley and the oldest girl appear as grownups in miniature overshadowed by the giant of their world, Gaoler Hawley. The family's diversions—battledore, horn book, nosegay, fan and doll—are all shown, while Mr. Hawley holds an open book containing either family or prisoners' accounts. Three romantic landscapes rich in castles and shepherds hang high on the walls; the floor is covered with a stenciled and painted floorcloth; fine eighteenth-century paneling is visible in wainscoting a door and inside window shutters. Two family portraits occupy the wall of an adjoining room; Mr. Hawley sits in a rush-seated ladder-back straight chair next to a small gate-leg tea table that appears to have been painted with elegant wood graining.

A small jewel is the watercolor portrait of *General Schumacker's Daughter* painted in Pennsylvania about 1812 (Fig. 109). Nearly as important as the pretty figure in profile is the background which further describes the subject. The perspective of the stenciled room, the chair, table and floor are set awry to show within one view the decorative order of the scene. Jacob Maentel, the artist, painted numerous full-length portraits of York, Lancaster, Lebanon and Berks County subjects between 1804 and 1837.

An artist identified only as Mr. Freeman painted the portrait of *Elizabeth Fenimore Cooper,* mother of James, (Fig. 110) in 1816 in her house on the shores of Lake Otesaga in Cooperstown, New York. The placid subject sits facing front, while the room becomes a stage setting for its star. But fine cabinetry in paneling and doorways, an abundance of plants in tidy tubs, a barometer above Windsor chairs and a drop-leaf table contribute to the delight of the scene. The floor, stenciled in squares, is echoed in the neat geometry of the striped wallpaper. The colors are complementary to the rich blue of Mrs. Cooper's gown.

The French hero of the Revolution, Lafayette, returned to America in triumph in 1824 and stayed until 1825. Country gentry vied with city officials and merchants to entertain him. The dark, contrasting figure in the finely decorated house of Moses Morse in Loudon, New Hampshire, has been identified as the Marquis (Fig. 111). French general or not, the house in which he stands is as splendid as the tall man. Color is varied from room to room and the walls of the best rooms are painted with stenciled and free-hand designs. The wood of the secretary, a unique example of cabinetmaking, echoes the warm Indian red and cream of the walls. The artist was Joseph Warren Leavitt of Chichester, New Hampshire.

Fantastic and gaudy in color and design, Mary Ann Willson's *Leavetaking* is a scene in which sentiment is subordinated to pattern (Fig. 112). Windows and figures are distorted in perspective and size, and the participants in the sentimental drama are set like cutouts against a bright poster, yet the angled windows and diminutive child dramatically emphasize the major figures in the scene.

101.

While men far outnumbered women as professional folk artists, at least one, Deborah Goldsmith, worked not only at home but traveled as an itinerant painter in search of patrons. In her most ambitious painting, *The Talcott Family* (Fig. 113), grandmother, father, mother, two children and the family dog are illustrated against a background that vibrates with design and color.

Typical of the delightful sprightliness of Joseph H. Davis' style is the portrait of *Mr. and Mrs. James Tuttle* (Fig. 114). Davis signed one of his watercolors "left-hand painter." Working in New Hampshire and Vermont in the 1830s, he created gay patterns and designs that dazzle the viewer more than the likenesses of his subjects. Mr. Tuttle's profession is emphasized in the pictured view of his sawmill outlined on the back wall by a green garland. The painted chairs and marbleized table are set on an exuberantly patterned carpet. The family cat, a Bible and a fruit ararngement resembling a still life, complete this small family social history. Individual portraits of other members of the family were created by the same artist at their home in Stratford County, New Hampshire.

In 1835, the year before the Tuttle family sat for their portrait in New Hampshire, the children of Nathan Starr were painted with greater realism by Ambrose Andrews in Middletown, Connecticut (Fig. 115). The painting is not only a guide to nineteenth-century children's games—battledore and shuttlecock and hoop and stick—but shows—through the wide open wood-paneled French doors—a splendid view of the family munition works that had provided guns and bayonets to Americans since the late eighteenth century. The factory is down a steep hill; on the steps leading from the house, a small garden blooms in pots. The portrait, with static figures of children arrested in motion, seems close to modern realistic painting.

An abundance of daffodils and roses bloom around a solemn child in *Picking Flowers* (Fig. 116). Cat and house balance tree and flower basket in a stiff, symmetrical composition in which—except for the arms and hands—each half of the girl's body and face is an exact mirror image of the other.

Many of the tedious and time-consuming jobs required to maintain life in frontier communities were shared labors that became entertainment for the participants. In an art in which static scenes are the rule, the exceptions are interesting. In *Flax Scutching* (Fig. 117), Linton Park depicts a lively scene in which a whole community takes part in the processes necessary to convert flax to linen thread. Armed with paddles, the group—dressed up by western Pennsylvania standards—engages in scutching the flax over upright boards set into the ground. It is almost a Flemish scene, translated to American soil and placed against a background of pioneer cabins. Park was a lumberjack; his trade is reflected in the piles of logs and the neatly felled tree in the foreground.

A quilting party of the late 1850s illustrates the final use for cloth scraps (Fig. 119). As lively as *Flax Scutching*, the *Quilting Party* is less original; it is based on an engraved illustration from Gleason's *Pictorial*. The unknown copyist has, however, stylized the original figures, who are clad in a wide range of bright colors. Painted chairs, a curious gun and powder holder and painted window shades add interest to a neighborhood party bent on completing one of the ugliest quilts ever to grace a dowry.

Fourth of July Picnic (Fig. 118), the great annual event of a small town, is captured in an assemblage of watercolor cutouts of an elegant company at South Weymouth, Massachusetts. The composition is signed by Susan Merrett who is known through this single work. To the modern eye, she achieves an almost surreal quality in her collage of holiday celebrants arranged in precise and undiminished ranks against a painted background. Real events as subjects for young ladies are rare, and this delightful assemblage combines the real and ideal.

Pictorial evidence of nineteenth-century musical entertainments are visible in illuminated music sheets, music books and musical instruments that are frequent accompaniments to portraits. In a beautiful design, a Negro musician dressed as a minstrel strums on a banjo—its neck distorted so that its curve is visible (Fig. 121).

An early prize fight, with its participants in teams of three, takes place in the open air; *Bare Knuckles* by George Hayes dates to about 1860 (Fig. 120). It probably represents one of the championships that were fought in secret, in defiance of the law in the United States before 1880. Many of the matches took place in towns divided by state lines so that the ring might be moved to suit the officials present. The endurance of the nineteenth-century fighter is demonstrated by the Sullivan-Kilrain bout in 1889, the last major bare knuckles fight in America, which lasted seventy-five rounds.

Preceded the same year by Herman Melville aboard the whaler, *Acushnet,* Benjamin Russell of New Bedford set sail in November, 1841, to recoup his fortunes on the *Kutusoff.* He was an old man by whaler's standards; and at thirty-seven he probably served as the cooper for the three and a half year voyage. In December, 1848, a splendid panorama, *A Whaling Voyage Round the World* (Fig. 122), was shown for the first time at Sears' Hall in New Bedford. The panorama, based on Russell's sketches of his journey, was done by Russell and Caleb B. Purrington, a "fancy painter" and a member of the Fairhaven painting firm of Purrington and Taber.

The panorama, eight and a half feet high, painted in tempera on cotton sheeting, was advertised as being three miles long; it was, in fact, a little less than a quarter-mile journey. Panoramas of popular subjects were created as evening entertainments. As they were displayed and slowly unrolled across a stage from side to side, skilled narrators would relate the story of their wonders. Unlike most, the Russell-Purrington panorama unreeled in a westward direction, despite the fact that the world journey took an eastward course. Showings of the wonders of whaling were so popular in the decades following its creation that some of the most engrossing scenes were worn out from frequent use.

The artist's subjects were most often drawn from actual events based on the real world. But in the romantic nineteenth century, drama had its role. Dreams or legends might inspire a painter to create scenes that are puzzling to the observer today. *Meditation by the Sea* is a small but somehow overwhelming canvas that gives this effect (Fig. 123). The tiny figure at lower left faces an apparent dilemma as an advancing tide washes toward him in stylized waves and surf. At his back is a high cliff, its upper reaches apparently inaccessible. Two figures walk the sands in the far distance, and farther still a huge, jagged rock divides the sand and the sea. The background is a calm sunlit sky and dark ocean where ships sail free. But one's attention is drawn to the figure in the foreground by the excitement of the surf that rushes toward him.

A dark runaway horse, bridled but unsaddled, seems endlessly escaping in a painting by an unknown artist (Fig. 124). A dream town on a river occupies the background in still beauty. The black horse pursued by a spotted dog is the center of interest in the restless foreground where trees, roots and plants repeat the design of the runaway's flowing mane.

The portrait painter often traveled to find his patrons; horses and carriages appear in portraits, genre scenes and landscapes, but few good painted representations on the rigors of the artists' travels in the nineteenth century are known.

Well past mid-century a rare western folk painting by Joseph Becker showed the mode of travel that finally served the itinerant painter in some comfort. Becker's *The First Transcontinental Train Leaving Sacramento, California—May 1869* (Fig. 125) illustrates not only the train itself, but some of the workmen—many of them oriental laborers—who laid the first cross-country track. Transportation within a city is shown in the view of New York's *Third Avenue Railroad Depot* by J. H. Schenk (Fig. 126).

FIG. 88. EDWARD HICKS. *Cornell Farm.* Oil, 1848.
National Gallery of Art,
collection of Edgar William and Bernice Chrysler Garbisch

FIG. 89. EDWARD HICKS. *Leedom Farm.* Oil, 1849. Abby Aldrich Rockefeller Folk Art Collection

FIG. 90. EDWARD HICKS. *The Residence of David Twining, 1787.* Oil, about 1846.
Abby Aldrich Rockefeller Folk Art Collection

FIG. 91. LEWIS MILLER.
Sketches from Lewis Miller's Notebooks.
Watercolor and ink, 1799-1807.
Historical Society of York County, York, Pennsylvania

FIG. 92. Artist unknown. *Old Plantation*. Watercolor, about 1800. Abby Aldrich Rockefeller Folk Art Collection

FIG. 93.   TERENCE J. KENNEDY. *Political Banner*. Oil, about 1840.
New York State Historical Association

FIG. 94. ALEXANDR BOUDRO(U). *A. Dickson Entering Bristol in 1819.*
Oil on wood panel, 1851.
Abby Aldrich Rockefeller Folk Art Collection

FIG. 95. Artist unknown. *Charlestown Prison*. Watercolor, about 1820.
Collection of Edith Gregor Halpert

FIG. 96. Artist unknown. *Darkytown*. Painting on glass, about 1870.
New York State Historical Association

FIG. 97. C. J. HAMILTON. *Market Square, Charleston.* Oil, about 1869.
Abby Aldrich Rockefeller Folk Art Collection

FIG. 98. EUNICE PINNEY. *Couple and Casualty.* Watercolor, about 1815.
Abby Aldrich Rockefeller Folk Art Collection

THE COTTERS' SATURDAY NIGHT

FIG. 99. EUNICE PINNEY. *The Cotter's Saturday Night.* Watercolor, about 1820.
Collection of Edgar William and Bernice Chrysler Garbisch

FIG. 100. EUNICE PINNEY. *Two Women.* Watercolor, about 1815.
New York State Historical Association

FIG. 101. **EUNICE PINNEY.** *Children Playing.* Watercolor, about 1815.
Abby Aldrich Rockefeller Folk Art Collection

FIG. 102. EUNICE PINNEY. *Death Memorial.* Watercolor, about 1815.
New York State Historical Association

FIG. 103. EUNICE PINNEY. *Mrs. Clarke the York Magnet.* Watercolor, 1821.
Abby Aldrich Rockefeller Folk Art Collection

FIG. 104. Artist unknown. *Mourning Picture for Philo Day.* Watercolor on silk, about 1810.
Abby Aldrich Rockefeller Folk Art Collection

FIG. 105. Artist unknown.
Polly Botsford and Her Children.
Watercolor, about 1815.
Abby Aldrich Rockefeller
Folk Art Collection

FIG. 106. Artist unknown.
Memorial to Daniel Ma. . . .
Watercolor, about 1801.
Abby Aldrich Rockefeller
Folk Art Collection

FIG. 107. R. FIBICH. *York Springs Graveyard*. Oil, about 1860.
New York State Historical Association

FIG. 108. WILLIAM WILKIE. *Nathan Hawley, and Family.* Watercolor, 1801.
Albany Institute of History and Art

FIG. 109. JACOB MAENTEL. *General Schumacker's Daughter.*
Watercolor, about 1812.
Collection of Edgar William and Bernice Chrysler Garbisch

FIG. 110. Mr. FREEMAN. *Elizabeth Fenimore Cooper.* Watercolor, 1816.
New York State Historical Association

FIG. 111. JOSEPH WARREN LEAVITT. *Interior of the Moses Morse House.*
Watercolor, 1825.
Collection of Nina Fletcher Little

FIG. 112. MARY ANN WILLSON. *Leavetaking*. Watercolor, about 1820.
Museum of Fine Arts, Boston, M. and M. Karolik Collection

FIG. 113. DEBORAH GOLDSMITH. *The Talcott Family*. Watercolor, 1832.
Abby Aldrich Rockefeller Folk Art Collection

FIG. 114. JOSEPH H. DAVIS. *Mr. and Mrs. James Tuttle.* Watercolor, 1836.
New-York Historical Society

FIG. 115. AMBROSE ANDREWS. *The Children of Nathan Starr.*
Oil, 1835.
Collection of Mr. and Mrs. Nathan Comfort Starr

FIG. 116. Artist unknown.
Picking Flowers. Oil, about 1845.
New York State Historical Association

FIG. 117. LINTON PARK. *Flax Scutching.* Oil, about 1860.
Collection of Edgar William and Bernice Chrysler Garbisch

FIG. 118. SUSAN MERRETT. *Fourth of July Picnic.* Watercolor, about 1845.
Art Institute of Chicago

FIG. 119. Artist unknown. *Quilting Party*. Oil on cardboard, about 1858.
Abby Aldrich Rockefeller Folk Art Collection

FIG. 120. GEORGE HAYES. *Bare Knuckles*. Oil, about 1860.
Collection of Edgar William and Bernice Chrysler Garbisch

FIG. 121. D. MORRILL. *Banjo Player*. Oil, 1862.
Wadsworth Atheneum

FIG. 122. BENJAMIN RUSSELL and CALEB PURRINGTON.

Original Panorama of a Whaling Voyage Round the World.
Tempera on cotton sheeting, 1848.
Old Dartmouth Historical Society and Whaling Museum

FIG. 123. Artist unknown. *Meditation by the Sea*. Oil, about 1855.
Museum of Fine Arts, Boston, M. and M. Karolik Collection

FIG. 124. Artist unknown. *Runaway Horse*. Oil, about 1840.
Former Whitney Collection

FIG. 125. JOSEPH BECKER. *The First Transcontinental Train Leaving Sacramento, California—May 1869.* Oil, 1869.
Gilcrease Institute

FIG. 126. J. H. SCHENK. *Third Avenue Railroad Depot*. Oil, about 1860.
Metropolitan Museum of Art

LANDSCAPE, SEASCAPE AND TOWNSCAPE

NINETEENTH-CENTURY TRAVELERS in America were astounded by the vastness and beauty of the new republic. While the astringent Mrs. Trollope found little that was good in the society and manners of Americans, the country itself was a marvel to which she gave unstinting praise.

She deplored the attitude of the nineteenth-century American whose philosophy, she accurately remarked, was, "I'm as good as you are." A new romanticism and a new republic together had created the cult of the individual, an influence that permeated every aspect of American society, thought and art. Emphasis on man, by nature a good and natural being, was a philosophy that was warmly accepted along the frontiers that had been howling wildernesses almost to the end of the colonial period. Far up the rivers from the falls nearest the rivers' mouths that had been the outposts of early colonization, the farmers of New England, New York and Pennsylvania embraced the new philosophy. These areas were the seed ground for utopian movements, religious revivalism and a new and typically native folklore. By his very presence the pioneer on uncultivated land was in revolt against authoritarianism; in these regions every man was king by right of the qualities that made him different from every other man in small, inbred, rural communities.

At the beginning of the nineteenth century the land itself was only beginning to respond to improved agrarian methods. As the century wore on the sons and daughters of these frontiersmen had time to record the wonders they saw in the newly cultivated and inhabited landscape. The southern plantation, the prosperous farms of Pennsylvania, the natural wonders of the new states, the land and towns of New York and New England and even the ships that plied the country's rivers and shores were subjects for self-taught artists.

Two plantation views show a contrast in approach. One, painted by an unknown artist on a wood panel (Fig. 127), is a highly stylized, flat and ornamental design. Susan Whitcomb's *Residence of General Washington* (Fig. 128), dated 1842, is a faithful replica of a copy of the engraving *Mount Vernon in Virginia* published by the artist Alexander Robertson and by Francis

Jukes in New York in 1800. Trees with feathery, exotic foliage frame both plantations at either margin, but there the resemblance ends.

The Plantation of about 1825 extends the fantasy in an arrangement that heightens the design. Pockets of sky and pond allow the outlines of a giant grapevine and a tiny willow and wildflowers to be seen clearly against a pale background. The high hill of the plantation, set to avoid the patterning of the trees, is crested by a great Federal manor; its dependencies wind down to the river's edge. There, a ferociously armed full-rigged ship sails amid patterned waves. There are touches of realism in a formal garden that separates the house from its outbuildings, and in an undershot water wheel that operates the mill at lower right.

Susan Whitcomb, a student at the Literary and Scientific Institution in Brandon, Vermont, exactly duplicated a painting that one of her teachers, Lovisa Chatterton Hammond, painted in 1816. In 1842 the Institution's advertisement listed instruction in painting "with the use of patterns" as an extra. It was an inexpensive extra, for lessons cost only a dollar each quarter, while laundry for the same period at the same school cost three times as much. Small wonder that so many girls learned to paint from sources given to them by their instructors.

The wide range of style in portraying the Pennsylvania landscape can be studied in an oil painting, *Twenty-Two Houses and a Church* (Fig. 129) and a watercolor, *Pennsylvania Farmstead with Many Fences* (Fig. 130). Buildings, trees and picket fences are common to each. In both instances houses are painted as flat cutouts with no attempt at perspective; but the country barn is rendered in a bird's-eye view. In the watercolor, fences are laid flat, forming a rigid pattern that divides the orderly scene. Only the barn and a marsh fenced off at upper left disrupt its angularity. In contrast to the stylized farmstead, green and white picket fences winding from left to right and a vine in outline against high white church walls give a curving rhythm to *Twenty-Two Houses and a Church*.

During his long career as an artist, Edward Hicks painted at least two versions of one of America's greatest wonders, the thundering *Falls of Niagara*, that had inspired artists and travelers from earliest days. Traditionally, one of the scenes was painted as a fireboard for the Philadelphia surgeon Joseph Parrish, who was the Hicks's family doctor (Fig. 131). The lower molding of the frame is new; the painting may once have been longer with cutouts to allow andirons to support the board in a closed-up fireplace. The general design for Hicks's composition is from Merigot's engraving after an oil painting by John Vanderlyn. But Hicks knew the Falls first-hand; he visited them in 1819 in the company of two friends, Isaac Parry and Mathias Hutchinson. Hicks painted the waterfall surrounded by trees in full autumn glory and added a serpent, moose, eagle and beaver. Couplets from Alexander Wilson's *The Foresters* surround the painting. The poem, by the famous Scotsman who became a leading American ornithologist, was reprinted in Newtown—Hicks's own town—in 1818.

Besides farms and nature's grandeur, houses and towns were subjects for folk artists. About 1830 an unidentified artist painted the house and shop

143.

of the chairmaker David Alling of Newark, New Jersey (Fig. 132). Two of Alling's chairs stand in front of his Broad Street address; the house is shown in starkly simplified form that suggests the work of Edward Hopper.

The interiors of houses were frequently enriched with stenciled or free-hand designs. A narrow hallway in the Old Cushman Tavern at Webster Corner, Maine, was painted about 1830 by Orison Wood (Fig. 133). It appears much wider than it is through clever use of a rapidly diminishing perspective. The wall painting was designed to fill the space completely; it is divided vertically with large exotic trees, while conventional and compact evergreens, far smaller than the giants in the foreground, carry the eye along a horizontal plane.

In the same tradition of simplified form filling space, but on a lesser scale than freehand wall painting, is *Exotic Landscape* (Fig. 134), a rich, somber painting by an unknown artist. A waterfall divided by two rocky prominences is at the center of the painting, but almost equal importance is given to large plants and a tree at the right—with branches like tentacles—and to a fountain in the lower left corner. The landscape may have been based on a real or print model, but in execution it appears as a romantic vision of the flora of the moon.

In contrast to exotic landscapes, the everyday world and its progress in scientific achievement were represented in portraits of American steam and sailing ships. The clipper ship *Golden West* was painted under full sail against an oriental pattern of waves that represents the Indian Ocean in 1862 (Fig. 135). Native fishing vessels are seen in the background; the artist's name, Charles Nissen, is inscribed on a keg floating at lower right. The clipper was built by Donald McKay and set a new record in the run between San Francisco and Japan; the ship painting was commissioned by the owners to commemorate the event. While the hull is distorted, the sails and rigging are seen in full splendor as the vessel heels over in the wind.

Contrasting with the exciting angle of the *Golden West,* static side views of river steamboats that brightened the nineteenth-century scene were portrayed by James and John Bard. The Bards, twins, were born in the Chelsea section of New York City in 1815. John died in 1856, leaving James to carry on a long career as a ship portraitist. A contemporary of James, Samuel Ward Stanton, placed his production at the astonishing figure of 4,000 compositions; the current total of known portraits by both of the Bards is about 375. James Bard died in White Plains but most of the Bards' working careers were spent in the city.

Only a few paintings are inscribed as the work of both artists. The divisions of labor between them is not known, but the gaiety and naïveté of the early pieces and the pale palette in oils suggest that James drew the boats from life and transferred the drawings to canvas; John probably supplied the color, figures and backgrounds. James, working on his own—the majority of oils and all the watercolors and pencil sketches are his—had a distinctive and appealing style. The ships are carefully described to scale; they were first measured and sketched from life in pencil. While the ships were accurate in every detail, the backgrounds, supplied later in the studio, were designed to complement and outline each vessel.

The steamboat *America* (Fig. 136), is one of several famous vessels that bore the same name; the portrait, set against a Hudson River background, is the work of James Bard. The *R. L. Stevens*, signed as the work of both James and John, dates to about 1835 (Fig. 137).

Bunkerhill (Fig. 138), painted by Frederick Huge in 1838, was probably done in Connecticut where the ship was built and where the artist worked seven years later. *R. L. Stevens* and *Bunkerhill* are almost identical walking beam side-wheelers, with twin stacks athwartships from boilers on the decks that overhang the ships' hulls. While the Bards show the *Stevens* realistically, it churns its way up the Hudson through a mass of ice that is probably greatly exaggerated, although horses and sleighs are seen on the ice near shore. The contrasting study of the *Bunkerhill* is a stylized design in which waves and smoke are transformed into interesting patterns.

The upper Hudson was the subject of a quaint fantasy by an unknown artist who used the round cover of a keg for his painting (Fig. 139). House-sized ducks and boat-sized grasses and flowers add to the rural view. At center ground a charming little summerhouse is a copy of a Greek temple.

An enchanting vision of *Lockport on Erie Canal* (Fig. 140), 1832, by Mary Keys is akin in its simple spirit to an unknown schoolgirl's *Venice* painted at about the same time (Fig. 141). The neatly geometric houses, canals and bridges and the gaily colored figures that ride a canal boat in New York State and gondolas in Venice are surprisingly similar.

The romantic vision of America's towns at mid-century is captured in two New York townscapes. *Eagle Mill* with its prominent factories and "double-barreled" covered bridge is portrayed as it appeared on a fair summer's day (Fig. 142). A painted border of grapes, vines and leaves surrounds the canvas. Painted within an oval on an octagonal wood panel is the town of *Poestenkill*, near Troy (Fig. 143). The winter view, that dates to about 1850, is by Joseph Hidley, the town's resident artist. It is one of a number of townscapes painted by him that show the town close up and far away and in every season of the year.

FIG. 127. Artist unknown. *The Plantation*. Oil on wood, about 1825. Metropolitan Museum of Art, collection of Edgar William and Bernice Chrysler Garbisch

FIG. 128. SUSAN WHITCOMB. *The Residence of General Washington.*
Watercolor, 1842.
Abby Aldrich Rockefeller Folk Art Collection

FIG. 129. Artist unknown.
Twenty-Two Houses and a Church.
Oil, about 1830.
National Gallery of Art,
collection of Edgar William
and Bernice Chrysler Garbisch

FIG. 130. Artist unknown. *Pennsylvania Farmstead with Many Fences.*
Watercolor, about 1830.
Museum of Fine Arts, Boston, M. and M. Karolik Collection

FIG. 131. EDWARD HICKS. *The Falls of Niagara*. Oil on wood, about 1835.
Abby Aldrich Rockefeller Folk Art Collection

FIG. 132. Artist unknown. *The House and Shop of David Alling*. Oil, about 1830.
Newark Museum

FIG. 133. ORISON WOOD. *Trees, Lake and Islands.* Fresco on plaster, about 1830.
Old Cushman Tavern, Webster Corner, Maine

FIG. 134. Artist unknown.
Exotic Landscape.
Oil, about 1845.
Abby Aldrich Rockefeller
Folk Art Collection

FIG. 135. CHARLES NISSEN. *Golden West*. Oil, 1868.
Abby Aldrich Rockefeller Folk Art Collection

FIG. 136. JAMES BARD. *America.* Oil, about 1850. Smithsonian Institution, Van Alstyne Collection

FIG. 137. JOHN and JAMES BARD. *R. L. Stevens.* Oil, about 1835.
Mariners Museum

FIG. 138. FREDERICK HUGE. *Bunkerhill*. Watercolor, 1838.
Mariners Museum

FIG. 139. Artist unknown. *Hudson River Landscape*. Oil on wood, about 1840.
Abby Aldrich Rockefeller Folk Art Collection

FIG. 140. MARY KEYS. *Lockport on Erie Canal.* Watercolor, 1832.
Munson-Williams-Proctor Institute

FIG. 141. Artist unknown. *Venice.* Watercolor, about 1835.
New York State Historical Association

FIG. 142. Artist unknown. *Eagle Mill.* Oil, about 1845.
Abby Aldrich Rockefeller Folk Art Collection

FIG. 143. JOSEPH HIDLEY. *Poestenkill—Winter.*
Oil on wood panel, about 1850.
Abby Aldrich Rockefeller Folk Art Collection

Colloquial History

THE AMERICAN FOLK ARTIST made little differentiation between contemporary history and Greek myths, between moral lessons of every day and Bible stories: each provided him with a subject. While history was portrayed in the light of surging patriotism and exciting religions, events historically or geographically near or far took on the character and flavor of the artist's environment. As a result Biblical lions sometimes became household tabbies, Indians greeted explorers in pink rompers and Washington, the undisputed hero of all, became a brash boy astride a great horse.

This is not to say that Biblical and national events were always reduced to the vocabulary of the marketplace or farmyard. Even though the Bible was translated to Bucks County or to an imaginary temple drawn in the pure Egyptian revival style, the need to restate the great stories in contemporary terms produced works of strength and merit. In the opposite vein, Washington drawn from life rarely looked as impressive as he did in folk artists' versions of his crossing of the Delaware or of his review of the Western Army. Every man had the potential—and the belief—that he or his son might be president; a religious society believed that its leader was God's daughter as Jesus was His son. In such a world anything was possible, and portrayals of great deeds and events followed the prevailing trend.

INSPIRATION FROM MAN

WHILE ALMOST EVERY GENRE SCENE or portrait was a direct or side comment on local, national or religious history, a large number of paintings by untutored artists were inspired directly by historical events. Nationalist fervor dictated that most of the subjects be based on American themes. *Christopher Columbus Landing upon the Island of St. Salvador* is copied from a print (Fig. 144). But the wonder and delight of the naïve rendering indicates some of the exhilaration that self-taught artists found in painting scenes from America's past. In tiny script at the top of the encircled view is written "Where Liberty dwells there is my Country." Squirrels and monkeys, as tame as the gentle natives, inhabit the abundant forest from which two Indians in bizarre costumes survey the landing scene. The welcoming of Columbus is hidden almost as well as the subject of Brueghel's *Fall of Icarus.* In the top margin a rampant eagle carries a banner above swords, flags and bayonets.

Beginning with the *Peacable Kingdom of the Branch,* a subject which Edward Hicks first painted about 1825, virtually all the *Kingdoms* contain a version of William Penn's treaty with the Indians. The treaty became part of Hicks's favorite theme because he believed that in Penn's "holy experiment" in Pennsylvania lay the seeds for fulfilling the Biblical prophecy of heaven on earth. The dates·during which the treaty scenes figure most prominently in the *Kingdoms* are the years when Hicks was painting *Penn's Treaty* as a separate subject (Fig. 145). The source that he copied with variations was an engraving by H. B. Hall after Benjamin West's painting. Because of the dazzling color in all of Hicks's treaties, wholly different from West's palette, and because of the reversed images, it seems unlikely that he ever saw the original. Hicks's literal-minded approach is shown in the plainly legible list of "signers" that varies slightly in several of the paintings.

Nine versions of *Penn's Treaty* by Hicks are known today. Although they differ from one another and from the source in figures, poses and costume details, the treaties may be divided into two general groups: versions approximately the same size as the smallest *Peaceable Kingdom* and painted on wood, and larger compositions on canvas with inscriptions boldly set beneath Hicks's familiar chasm of eroded earth.

Hicks never overcame his problems with anatomy, even though he used prints to guide him in portraying people. Yet, the dark Indians with over-large heads and wooden gestures are in contrast to his painstaking attempts to give true likenesses of William Penn and the circle of Friends who surround him.

Hicks painted at least six versions still known today of *Washington Crossing the Delaware* based on a popular engraving after an oil completed by Thomas Sully in 1819. In Hicks's copies the only departure from the original composition is a quarter moon shining out from a stormy sky. The versions are dated early, midway and late in Hicks's career, and exhibit marked variations in technique.

Washington Crossed Here from Hicks's middle age is one of two similar canvases that are supposed to have hung at either end of a covered bridge that spanned the Delaware at Washington's Crossing (Fig. 146). The painting was rescued, according to an old museum catalog, just before the bridge was swept away by a flood in 1841.

In December, 1776, Washington and his troops encamped on the outskirts of Hicks's later home at Newtown. All Christmas day, the ragged troops—whose agreed enlistment period was, in more than half that army, due to run out—filed to the banks of the Delaware. There they were ferried across the river on Christmas night by John Glover's amphibious force of Marblehead fishermen in their own boats. Following the attack on Trenton the army returned to Newtown to gain strength for the renewed attack on Cornwallis early in 1777.

But before their return to Trenton, Washington's men and the British on their way to aid Cornwallis engaged in the battle of Princeton. John Trumbull sketched the scene, and John Mercer, the deaf-mute son of the American General Hugh Mercer, recorded his own version shortly after his father's death from a mortal wound received in the battle. Fifty years later, M. M. Sanford copied a print and painted the murderous charge of American mounted and foot soldiers against the British in a primitive view of the battle at the moment of Mercer's fall (Fig. 147).

In a nation newly at peace the General and his "Ledy" were portrayed by an artist identified only by his style (Fig. 148). *Excelenc Georg General Waschingdon and Ledy Waschingdon* appear in a small watercolor in which design and color lend enchantment to the drawing. A handful of drawings are attributed to the unknown artist, all of them showing women with net headdresses that lead to his identification as the "bee bonnet" fractur maker. In this painting, the best known of his works, space is used with great economy and inventiveness. The composition is carefully planned so that the figures strongly dominate the area inside the decorated border. The formal stance of the figures reduces fame to fable and the title echoes the guttural pronunciation of the Pennsylvania Germans. Imaginative and gay, the watercolor of General and Mrs. Washington uses a traditional European form to interpret familiar American history in a fresh idiom.

On October 18, 1794, Washington reviewed the Western Army at Fort Cumberland on the Potomac, the easternmost fort established during the French and Indian War. In a clean, powerful portrait, the Baltimore painter Frederick Kemmelmeyer recorded the scene (Fig. 149). Washington is seen close up astride a white horse as he moves toward the battalions standing in ranks before the encampment. All emphasis is on the equestrian figure outlined against diminutive troops and the fort. The scene that was painted took place almost one month to the day before Jay's Treaty which established the power of the new nation and its president by securing northwestern outposts against British occupation; Washington is depicted here as the legendary hero he was to become for the American folk painter.

In contrast to Kemmelmeyer's portrayal is another *General Washington on Horseback* by Mary Ann Willson (Fig. 151); he looks like a cardboard figure astride a cardboard steed. A pistol's bang is indicated by a circle of smoke from its barrel, and sprightly dots and dashes pattern saddle blanket and harness. Squiggles of color in the background set the figure in space. This is a delightfully primitive version of a popular subject.

With equal charm *Miss Liberty* is posed holding palms of peace in one hand and supporting the flag and a liberty cap atop a pole in the other (Fig. 150). She is dressed in clocked stockings and an embroidered muslin dress (the embroidery expressed in pin pricks from the reverse of the paper). The watercolor, by an unknown artist, is initialed "F" in the lower corner; the maker considered herself less important than the patriotic inscription.

An imposing, portly military man identified as *General Schumacker* is the subject of a small incisive portrait in pen and watercolor (Fig. 154). The painting is a masterpiece by Jacob Maentel. In addition to the detailed profile figure and Maentel's characteristic hillocks and leafy foliage, the General holds a battle plan while a miniature battle—as if between toy soldiers—takes place in the background amid whirling smoke. The uniforms are of the period of the War of 1812, and Schumacker may be the Peter Shoemaker who was inspector of the second brigade of Bucks County in the War of 1812.

In contrast to subjects of national pride is a schoolgirl's version of the *Entry of Napoleon into Paris from Elba 1814* (Fig. 153). Painted by an unknown artist about 1825, it is a copy of the frontispiece of *Memoirs of the Military and Political Life of Napoleon* by Dr. B. E. O'Meara, printed in Hartford in 1822. The original engraving was by Isaac Sanford, also of Hartford. In the copy, decorated at the top margin with a rose, Napoleon is set before a village in a carriage drawn by white horses. Miniature horsemen greet the returning general; it looks like a scene created with Alpine toys and block villages.

Like dolls, too, are the highly stylized provincial figures of the Centre County, Pennsylvania, artist identified as H. Young. At least once, Young's small-footed, small-handed pair, which he painted many times, are removed from the country and identified as personages of national importance, *General Jackson and his Lady* (Fig. 152). Jackson toasts the future just as the gentlemen do who decorate the family records of Young's Pennsylvania neighbors.

With the color and excitement characteristic of battle scenes by folk artists, an unidentified battle between the blue and gray was sketched by an unknown artist (Fig. 155). Casualties occupy a great part of the scene which depicts a Union charge against a Confederate stand. The subject was probably copied after the war from a sketch or magazine illustration; the Civil War was extensively recorded not only by the camera, but by a number of battle artists working on the scene.

FIG. 144. Artist unknown. *Christopher Columbus Landing upon the Island of St, Salvador.* Watercolor, about 1825.
New York State Historical Association

FIG. 145.   EDWARD HICKS. *Penn's Treaty with the Indians.* Oil on wood panel,
about 1830.
Abby Aldrich Rockefeller Folk Art Collection

FIG. 146. EDWARD HICKS. *Washington Crossed Here*. Oil, about 1834.
Collection of Nina Fletcher Little

FIG. 147. M. M. SANFORD. *Washington at Princeton*. Oil, 1850.
New York State Historical Association

FIG. 148. Artist unknown. *Excelenc Georg General Waschingdon and Ledy Waschingdon.* Watercolor, about 1785.

Abby Aldrich Rockefeller Folk Art Collection

FIG. 149. FREDERICK KEMMELMEYER. *General George Washington.*
Reviewing the Western Army at Fort Cumberland. Oil, about 1795.
Henry Francis du Pont Winterthur Museum

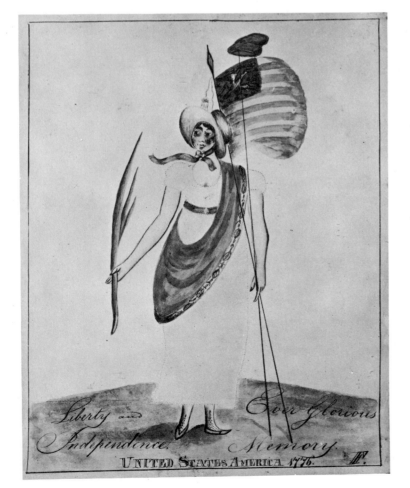

FIG. 150. Artist unknown.
Miss Liberty. Watercolor, about 1815.
Abby Aldrich Rockefeller Folk Art Collection

FIG. 151. MARY ANN WILLSON. *General Washington on Horseback.*
Watercolor, about 1820.
Museum of Art, Rhode Island School of Design

FIG. 152. Attributed to H. Young.
General Jackson and his Lady. Watercolor,
about 1825.
Museum of Fine Arts, Boston,
M. and M. Karolik Collection

FIG. 153. Artist unknown. *Entry of Napoleon into Paris from Elba 1814.*
Watercolor, about 1825.
Abby Aldrich Rockefeller Folk Art Collection

FIG. 154. JACOB MAENTEL. *General Schumacker.*
Watercolor and pen, about 1812.
Collection of Edgar William and Bernice Chrysler Garbisch

FIG. 155. Artist unknown. *Civil War Battle*. Oil, about 1870.
National Gallery of Art,
collection of Edgar William and Bernice Chrysler Garbisch

INSPIRATION FROM GOD

HISTORY PAINTING by untutored artists took on a domesticity that reduced national events to the scale of the rural homestead. Religious subjects, too, were made of everyday stuff with only an occasional flight to grand ideas and themes. The treatment was typical of the spirit of the Second Great Awakening of evangelistic religion, a movement that surged and ebbed in America from 1800 to the 1850s. The religious revival was an idea as compatible to the mind and heart of the average man as artistic creation. To people isolated on farms or in small towns a vital belief in God was a triumph that was local rather than national. Victories over sin and the Devil were fought in the smallest meeting places. To the ordinary man, the conquest was no less worthwhile because the battleground was small; the community was the world in microcosm. This was no mission to the foreign heathen but a battle fought in each social unit, the victory of noble pioneers reforming their peers and neighbors.

Romanticism flourishing in creative form vanquished the rationalism of colonial arts, politics and society. Ever-present death, sin, immorality, intemperance and slavery were all fuel to religious endeavors. A literal vision of God and the saints could be recorded by members of a religious community; a coach painter turned artist reduced his inner frustration in painting compositions laden with personal symbolism.

The excitement of evangelism flourished between wars and national crises as an escape from everyday routine. Little wonder that religious themes were favored by folk painters; they suited their taste and temperament and were creative, often reverent expressions of the times.

In some artists' hands even the most savage of Bible stories were reduced to the parlance of the common man. Jephthah's return home from victory in war and his fateful meeting with his daughter at the doors to his house are presented, not as a promised sacrifice to the Lord, but as a blithe scene combining elements from many sources (Fig. 156). Simply painted, the landscape suggests an embroidery of a New England scene; Jephthah's daughter and her companions are dressed in the style of the period and step forth from a portico that might have been borrowed from an early Renaissance annuncia-

171.

tion. The Moorish Gothic temple, a folly built at Stowe in the English countryside at Buckinghamshire, occupies the left background; Jephthah is a knight in white armor. The sacrifice is in the placid terms of daily life. The innocent combining of sources suggests that the artist, Betsy B. Lathrop, was a young and talented schoolgirl.

Strikingly similar in concept is another composition, *The Royal Psalmist* by Lucy Douglas (Fig. 157). Painted about 1810, the setting and seated woman—even her neoclassic chair—are typical of New England. Only David, the psalmist, seated at center retains his Old Testament character. A winged figure surrounded by clouds completes the mysterious trio of musicians. Once more, watercolor imitates difficult and time-consuming stitchery. Bold linear elements appear in David's robe, are repeated in the strings of his harp and again in the small draped tent that outlines the figure of a girl. The whole concept of the watercolor indicates a naïve and a reverent spirit so familiar with the Bible that the New England locale seems appropriate even for the bearded king.

In contrast to the simplicity of *Jephthah's Return* and *The Royal Palmist*, another religious painting is a fiercely bold and energetic rendition of the parable of the Prodigal Son (Fig. 158). One of four illustrations of the story by Mary Ann Willson, *The Prodigal Son Reclaimed* is based on American engravings issued by Amos Doolittle in 1814. The prints transport the scene to New England, but in her renditions, Mary Ann Willson creatively changes the natural elements to alternately sharp and staccato patterns that transform the parable to a study in primitive style. Flat two-dimensional form and vivid color forecast the art of the modern avant-garde. An anonymous nineteenth-century letter writer, who provided all the facts known concerning the artist, records Miss Willson's own high opinion of her work.

Inspiration for religious folk art came not only from printed sources but from heaven itself. Messages were transmitted from paradise to living "instruments," members of the celibate and communal Believers in Christ's Second Appearing. They recorded the events of the Shaker revival that lasted for twenty years from the late 1830s to the late 1850s.

The Shaker prophetess Mother Ann Lee died in the first Shaker community at Watervliet, New York, in 1784. But in 1837 her second coming was forecast by a group of schoolgirls in the same community. Meeting for instruction, the girls suddenly began to shake and whirl. Later that August night, three of the girls fell into trancelike states in which they described celestial journeys guided by angels and heavenly spirits. Soon older children experienced the spirit seizures and in a few weeks they spread to the adult members of the community.

At New Lebanon, the Shakers' "Holy Mount," the leaders of the sect waited impatiently for a sign of Mother Ann's return to earth, and here, on a Sunday afternoon early in the spring of 1838, the new "work" began. Philemon Stewart, one of the guiding Church Order, was helped into meeting by two brethren. Moved as an instrument of Mother Ann and Jesus Christ he delivered a message direct from the heavenly throne; "the windows of heaven and the avenues of the spirit world [were] set open."

In the decade of Mother Ann's second appearance, and for a few years following, inspirational messages, spiritual presentations and divine revelations abounded. Physical evidences of this exuberant and joyful revival remain today in the inspirational drawings created then as gifts. Most of the drawings were done by sisters of the order, although the Shaker limners are seldom identified by name.

Since Shaker millennial laws expressly forbade ornament or display in architecture, handcraft or dress, the Shakers groped for ways to show a vision of a heaven where precious gems, golden crowns, full-blown roses, jeweled weapons and tables set with the finest dishes abounded. Slowly and tentatively, decorative devices were added to unadorned calligraphic descriptions—crowns and harps, roses, drums, stars and altars (Fig. 159). Amid the borders and ornaments decorating written messages from the Almighty Father or Mother Ann, one senses that the scribes glanced back over their shoulders now and again to see if the elders and ministry approved of this departure from Mother Ann's Gospel statutes.

Apparently they did. And because they did, the size, number and complexity of the compositions increased, and a symmetrical, symbolic, innocent art form flowered in the Shaker communities (Fig. 160). Delicate drawings and fine penmanship were traced in colored inks; the records dictated by Shaker mediums were illustrated with objects that were parts of their visions.

Inscriptions on the drawings reveal an artist's eye for fresh detail. Hannah Cahoon's inscription for *Tree of Light* reads: "The bright silver color'd blaze streaming from the edges of each green leaf resembles so many bright torches" (Fig. 161). The drawing itself, bright with color, is a delicately balanced tracery of branches and leaves.

The creation of inspirational drawings continued in tranquillity for a time after the excitement of Mother Ann's reappearance abated. But before 1860 the vital fire of the Shaker revival had dwindled to a spark. As a reminder of these wondrous days the drawings remain. The Shakers themselves were forbidden to display them on their walls and many spirituals survive in prime condition because they were carefully preserved in chests and boxes. The drawings are a true expression of a little known but divinely inspired folk art.

In 1858 and 1859, a third wave of religious enthusiasm swept the country; its relation to the rising tide of causes that led to the Civil War might be effectively argued. In Massachusetts it provided inspiration to a folk artist who had lost his vocation as a portrait painter to the all-seeing eye of the camera. Returning to his home in the Connecticut Valley after long years spent in New England and New York as an itinerant painter, Erastus Salisbury Field turned to religious themes. In the 1860s farming his own and his cousin's land in the little settlement along the Connecticut River called Plumtrees provided a meager existence, but subject pieces based on the Bible lifted him up and away from this humdrum life. Sobersided Yankee neighbors were not inclined to buy these paintings of fanciful visions to hang alongside the artist's strict early portraits of themselves, and his income from painting dwindled to almost nothing.

But as gifts for friends and relatives or for the Congregational Church in North Amherst, paintings of Eden's garden and Egypt's plagues seemed suitable. Field painted his impression of *The Garden of Eden* twice (Fig. 162). In depicting his sprightly, naïve view showing Eve at the moment of her temptation, Field borrowed and combined at least three versions of the scene into one. A Bible illustration of *The Temptation,* after a painting by the English artist John Martin, probably set the general composition; a print of *The Garden of Eden* after Thomas Cole gave additional details—a small waterfall and exotic plants seen at the right and left foreground. Finally, the animals paired in a Bible illustration after Jan Brueghel the Elder inspired the addition of paired creatures in both of Field's versions. The smaller of the two has a trompe l'oeil painted frame. Until restoration in this century, Eve and the serpent had been painted out in the larger version. Whether Field did this himself as a bow to Victorian prudishness is a matter for conjecture.

The color is bright and pleasing and the draftsmanship is that of an artist finding solutions to problems on his own. These elements are carried over to a series of large paintings of the Plagues of Egypt. Inspiration again came from Bible illustrations after John Martin and another English artist Richard Westall. But translated by Erastus Field in his fiftieth year as a self-taught artist the sources all but vanished in exuberant color, exotic architecture and boldly gesturing figures who closely resemble daguerreotypes of Field's neighbors and relatives (Fig. 163).

Not far removed from Plumtrees, over the Massachusetts–New York line, the far younger artist, Joseph Hidley, was at work. Although most of his paintings were minutely detailed townscapes of Poestenkill, New York, and the surrounding area, he suited his subject to the religious fervor of the late 1850s and created a handful of Biblical pictures. His *Noah's Ark* is painted on a wood panel with an arched top (Fig. 164). It presents an imaginative flight of romantic fancy in paired creatures and a tropical landscape that surround a dreamlike Ark. Besides his vocation as a painter, Hidley worked as a cabinetmaker and taxidermist. The wooden aspect of the animals marked for salvation might have been copied straight from his stuffed specimens.

In a landscape as moody as his own inner life, Edward Hicks evoked a version of the Ark and Flood that was modeled after an 1844 print by Nathaniel Currier, a copy still owned by Hicks's descendants. In one of the few references to painting contained in his *Memoirs,* Hicks, in his entry for April 18, 1846, joked that he was a smarter workman than Noah in his ability to build an ark faster (Fig. 165). His levity was short-lived; the same day he dismissed himself as "nothing but a poor worthless insignificant painter." Although the composition of *Noah's Ark* is modeled closely after the lithograph, the trees, shrubs and lowering sky, the surging color and the design and pattern of the animals transcend the source and make this one of Hicks's most beautiful works.

The theme that Hicks illustrated with many variations was the Biblical prophecy from Isaiah. The paintings dealt basically—as the prophecy did—

174.

with God's peaceable kingdom on earth; the lion would lie down with the lamb and the wild and domestic creatures would be led in peace by a child.

Approximately fifty-five versions of the *Peaceable Kingdom* by Hicks are known today, each differing slightly from the other. They show increasing technical ease as he learned to overcome difficulties with anatomy and form. Hicks's use of oil was consistently good—the paint is thin, the color crisp and clear.

In four versions the Natural Bridge of Virginia looms over a vignette showing *Penn's Treaty with the Indians* transplanted to a grassy mound by the stream that flows under the bridge (Fig. 166). Natural Bridge resembles a colored print of the scene made in London in 1808. From the slanted, vine-wrapped tree in the center to the rock surrounded by flowering plants at center foreground, no other example follows Richard Westall's version so closely; Westall's painting was reproduced as an illustration in countless editions of English and American Bibles.

The schism of 1827 dividing the Quakers into Orthodox ranks and Hicksites—followers of Edward's cousin Elias—led to an era in which the artist's personal anguish and involvement are visible in his *Kingdoms*. But by 1840 Hicks had found some degree of peace, and eight paintings on the theme he made so familiar date to that period; they show a gentleness and placidity lacking in the versions of the 1830s (Fig. 167). In the 1840 versions the creatures dominate the scene although *Penn's Treaty* (copied from a print after West) remains to remind one and all that Penn's Holy Experiment is Hicks's ideal of heaven on earth, while the restless creatures on the right represent man as he is, both good and evil. In these middle *Kingdoms* an emblematic figure frequently appears accompanied by an eagle and a dove. The woman feeding the eagle from a cup held in her outstetched hand is vaguely derivative from the late eighteenth-century painting of *Liberty as the Goddess of Mercy* by Edward Savage. Figures of two children come from yet another source, a French print that once hung in the painter's house in Newtown.

Liberty, a casual theme in some *Peaceable Kingdoms*, is dominant in the only paintings of peace by Hicks in which the treaty scene is missing. In the six versions known today Hicks illustrates an idea suggested in an exchange of long poems between the painter and his Bucks County neighbor, also a Friend, Samuel Johnson. The ideal world is a group of famous personages holding aloft a long banner; they represent progress toward the achievement of liberty in America.

In the *Peaceable Kingdoms* that date to the last five years of his life, the Quaker artist's own awareness of the approaching end of his earthly existence marks the canvases (Fig. 168). The children and creatures no longer shun the unknown den that yawns mysteriously in the *Kingdoms* painted between 1825 and 1840. Leopard, young goat and innocent child play or lie in the pit itself as though it were a sheltering haven. The creatures and children of God's kingdom wander peacefully from foreground into middle ground.

The stilted and stereotyped animals of the many *Kingdom*s from earlier series are replaced by new beasts arranged in open compositions that give a sense of serenity, order and depth to these last paintings. An arched and protective leopard stands over his mate who lies content in her den. Heavy-footed bulls, old and placid, stand by contented as cows. A calm, timeless and unmoving light floods the canvases suggesting Hicks's acceptance of old age and death.

In the note that accompanied the 1844 *Kingdom* painted for Dr. Joseph Watson (Fig. 169) Hicks identified it as ". . . one of the best paintings I ever done (& it may be the last)." It cost twenty dollars; the painter charged an extra $1.75 for a "fraim with ten coats of Varnish," made by his assistant Edward Trego.

In 1865, twenty-seven years after Hicks worked on his last *Peaceable Kingdom,* another Quaker, Dr. William Hallowell of Norristown, Pennsylvania, drew a fantasy on the same theme (Fig. 170). The conception seems modern and exciting. The creatures are encompassed by a womblike border imaginatively shown as plants, roots and trees; the animals are marked in exotic patterns, almost like anatomical studies.

FIG. 156. BETSY B. LATHROP. *Jephthah's Return.* Gouache, 1812.
Abby Aldrich Rockefeller Folk Art Collection

FIG. 157. LUCY DOUGLAS. *The Royal Psalmist*. Watercolor, about 1810.
Collection of Edith Gregor Halpert

FIG. 158. MARY ANN WILLSON. *The Prodigal Son Reclaimed*.
Watercolor, about 1820.
Collection of Edgar William and Bernice Chrysler Garbisch

FIG. 159. Attributed to Mary Hazard. *A Present from Mother Ann to Mary H.*
Watercolor, 1845.
Hancock Shaker Village

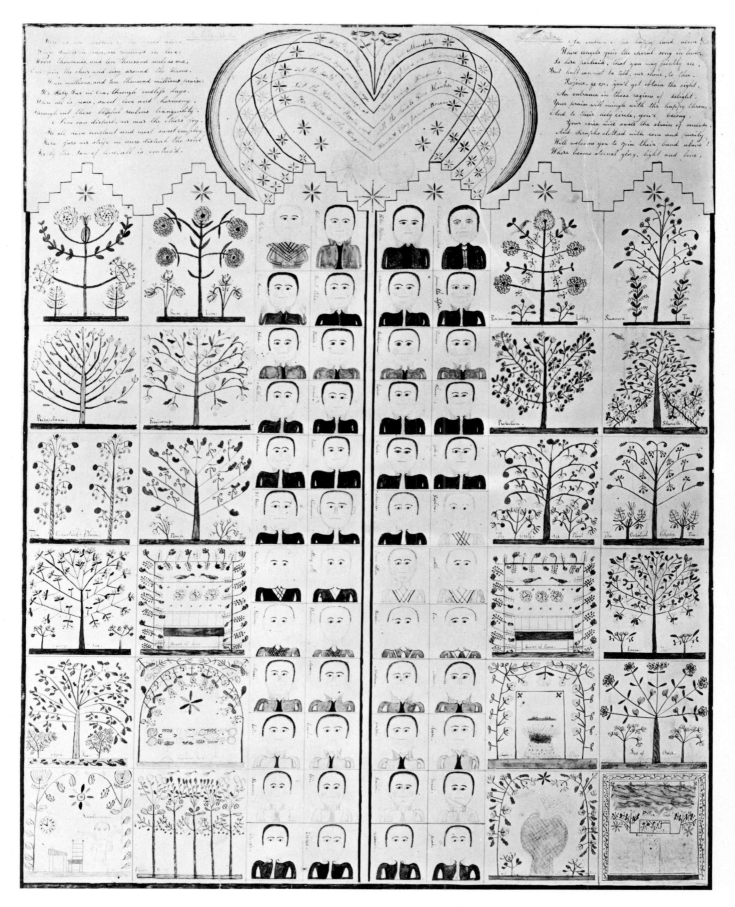

FIG. 160. Artist unknown. *An Emblem of the Heavenly Sphere.*
Watercolor, about 1854.
Hancock Shaker Village

FIG. 161. HANNAH CAHOON. *Tree of Light.* Watercolor, 1845. Hancock Shaker Village

FIG. 162. ERASTUS SALISBURY FIELD. *The Garden of Eden.*
Oil, about 1865.
Shelburne Museum

FIG. 163. ERASTUS SALISBURY FIELD. *Death of the First Born*. Oil, about 1875.
Collection of Edgar William and Bernice Chrysler Garbisch

FIG. 164. JOSEPH HIDLEY. *Noah's Ark*. Oil on wood panel, about 1855.
Abby Aldrich Rockefeller Folk Art Collection

FIG. 165. EDWARD HICKS. *Noah's Ark*. Oil, 1846.
Philadelphia Museum of Art

FIG. 166. EDWARD HICKS. *Peaceable Kingdom of the Branch.*
Oil on wood panel, about 1825.
Yale University Art Gallery

FIG. 167. EDWARD HICKS. *Peaceable Kingdom.* Oil, about 1840.
Collection of Mrs. Holger Cahill

FIG. 168. EDWARD HICKS. *Peaceable Kingdom*. Oil, 1844.
Abby Aldrich Rockefeller Folk Art Collection

FIG. 169. Edward Hicks's note
to Dr. Joseph Watson accompanying
the 1844 *Kingdom*.
Abby Aldrich Rockefeller Folk Art Collection

FIG. 170. WILLIAM HALLOWELL. *Peaceable Kingdom.* Pen and ink, 1865.
New York State Historical Association.

Art Instructor and Fractur Maker

DEVOUT PENNSYLVANIA MINISTERS, itinerant scribes, romantic schoolgirls and trained instructors were responsible for a vast bounty of American folk art. Most frequently, the strangely assorted group used pen, ink, pencil and watercolor, although young women were trained in the use of oils as well.

The creations of these artists, provincial and naïve, were not expressions of a united people sprung forth rootless on American ground. In their works the accent varied with the provenance. If the artist was a member of a culture transplanted intact from Europe, as was the scribe who made records for Pennsylvania Germans, his inspiration from the peasant art of his homeland was plain. The emphasis might be English if the artist worked as teacher or student in New England.

One of the traits held in common by these painters was more training in their avocation or craft than was granted to most folk artists. The itinerant scribe in Pennsylvania who took over the creation of family records almost exclusively after 1800 was frequently a skilled draftsman and colorist. At the same time, other northern states gave employment and encouragement to talented instructors who taught young women the delicate art of painting.

The scribe was occasionally a schoolmaster and both he and his counterpart teaching in New England and New York were consistently sound in the techniques they passed on to their students. Watercolor was employed to best advantage. Only occasionally were the pigments or inks so galling that papers were eaten away. Only rarely was the paint so thick that it flaked from its support. Generally, practice and technique were good.

The colors were sometimes ground and prepared by the artists themselves in plain water or in a tempered vehicle. Amateurs and women artists most often used boxes of prepared paint in which the cakes of color were molded or embossed with American eagles or British lions.

The papers vary widely from thin, translucent vellum to thick, handmade rag papers. The paints and the papers dictated the small size, and the fragile, ephemeral quality of the finished works is exemplified by *Watch and Fob* by J. A. Tilles (Fig. 171).

Each painting was a colorful testimonial to the reigning philosophy of the pioneers that made the creation and possession of paintings as commonplace to the middle class as it was to the aristocracy. If the rich could afford portraits and decorations and family records, the farmer and small-town shopkeeper could enjoy the same privilege.

In all the paintings by members of this large group of artists, romantic idealism is favored over realism, iconic likenesses over the actual, visions of heaven over the small commonplace adventures of everyday life.

THE ILLUMINATOR

IN PENNSYLVANIA numerous emigrants from Germany maintained their culture as members of Calvinistic or Pietist religions. Except for Moravians who established and continued high standards of education, the Germans and Swiss who composed a large part of Pennsylvania's population were isolated from intellectual pursuits and the main progress of life and thought in the new country. The illuminated manuscripts of the Pennsylvania Germans, produced in quantity from the middle of the eighteenth century to the eve of the Civil War, remain as evidence of these culturally isolated people who industriously farmed the rich fields of their adopted state.

Beautifully lettered and decorated texts were written in crude German; the language was corrupted further by an intermixture of dialects and by phonetic spelling. Magic, superstition and symbols from pagan and Christian sources were filtered through the medieval world and brought directly to Pennsylvania uninfluenced by the ideas of the Renaissance.

In this century the word fractur has come to be applied to the writing copies, family records, house blessings and decorative designs of the Pennsylvania Germans. In the strictest sense, the original word, *Fraktur,* applied only to illuminated manuscripts in which letters were modeled after the old type known as German Gothic.

The earliest examples of fractur writing were subtly colored and finely drawn illustrations of copy and song books, miracle plays and community records made by the celibate nuns and brethren of the cloister founded by Conrad Beissel at Ephrata, Pennsylvania. By the late eighteenth century the Ephrata community had vanished; its influence remained in fragmentary form in illuminated manuscripts by ministers, schoolteachers or writing masters who were Calvinists, Lutherans or members of the less worldly sect of Mennonites. The Moravians, who arrived in 1734, established themselves in Lehigh and Northampton Counties and promptly added their influence to Pennsylvania-German art. As the eighteenth century ended, Mennonite arts continued to develop and the influence of the late newcomers, the Schwenkfelders, became greater in the nineteenth century than in the eighteenth. The Lutherans and Calvinists continued to illuminate records. Symbols became contemporary and less secular than the medieval designs employed earlier.

With ink and translucent watercolor, an unknown Pennsylvania artist created a highly decorative drawing lettered in German script and celebrating the return of spring with its flowers (Fig. 172). A flowering vine set in a colorful jug dominates the painting which dates to about 1785. Bright figures dressed in red, blue, yellow and brown neatly fill the space and balance the composition.

A delightful scene in miniature was created in 1795 to honor the birthday of Jacob Van Vleck, minister and musician in the Moravian town of Bethlehem (Fig. 173). Van Vleck stands at the keyboard to play for a quintet of girls who are probably students at the Bethlehem Boarding School, of which he is Inspector. The romantic wreath of flowers that surrounds the musicians suggests that the artist may have been one of the schoolgirls although the celebrant's relative, William Van Vleck, was a student at nearby Nazareth Hall in 1799; a dozen years later, he made a watercolor of a Bethlehem scene.

Two similar paintings contain no calligraphy and are delightful illustrations of a lovers' meeting and a parable from the Bible. Both are by unknown illuminators, but rigid poses and brilliant color demonstrate primitive talents at work. *The Prodigal Son Reveling with Harlots* (Fig. 174) shows the wayward youth and a companion in uniforms of the 1790s. Chairs and a table are those commonly used late in the century, and the dresses of the ladies of the evening—flowered and small-figured striped chintzes—fit nicely into the contemporary setting for the parable. A winsome cat ignores the scene from its place on the low shelf of the serving table. About twenty years later than this illustration of the Bible is *Tryst on Ephrata Bridge* (Fig. 175). The meeting is outlined by a ruled and decorated margin; the scene looks almost like the start of a slow pavan on a miniature stage in Pennsylvania.

Unusual in its English text and American symbolism is the *Sarah Harley Birth Record* by John Van Minian; it was made to commemorate the child's birth in 1791 (Fig. 176). Like other records by Van Minian, an adaptation of the Great Seal of the United States appears at top center. Hearts in each corner contain a doggerel version of the building of Solomon's temple described in the First Book of *Kings*. The rhyming of "miss" with "brass," and "patterns" phonetically rendered as "Pattrens" extends the rough language used by fractur makers from German into English.

Perhaps the finest example of a Pennsylvania-German illuminated manuscript is the *Vorschrift* (Fig. 177), made by Reverend George Geistweite of Centre County, Pennsylvania, in 1801. A traveling minister and schoolmaster, the Reverend Geistweite produced a precise and beautiful fractur that closely followed those of Germany. The traditional intermixture of Christian and pagan symbols is retained in the leaping deer, pelican, tulip, peacock, lion and double-headed eagle which illustrate a verse from the Thirty-Fourth Psalm. The intricate design of this beautiful model of script is executed with great delicacy and care.

One of the fracturs created along Pennsylvania's eastern border was an 1818 New Year's Day gift for Elizabeth, wife of Peter Fedderly (Fig. 178). The figures are dressed in the old fashions of the late eighteenth century. A paunchy violinist serenades Mrs. Fedderly below a banner—in English—that proclaims the gift. A large figure in profile taps to the tune at the right, balanced by another large figure at far left.

The tulip appears as a symbol in a number of fracturs. In a purely decorative painting, tulips with large and small leaves and blossoms fill nearly all the space of a delicate watercolor (Fig. 179). In the lower quarter of the composition, a striped basket occupies the space; the tulips and leaves spring from it like sparks and flames.

Two artists, believed to be father and son, H. Young and the Reverend Young, worked in Centre County and surrounding areas in the nineteenth century. The older of the two men, H. Young, first created a composition that his son later followed with variations. The father shows profile figures of a man and woman facing each other above a small table with tripod feet. A decanter rests on the tabletop and the man toasts the lady with a glass of wine. These highly styled figures were repeated almost exactly by the son substituting a bouquet and nosegay for the decanter and glass. The Young watercolors were usually inscribed as family records. This version, however, is unique; it is inscribed for Miss Frances Taylor and just below the name, in a prominent position, is the vital fact, "Picture Bought A.D. 1831" (Fig. 180).

Another conscientiously inscribed document was a present for Catherine Smith of Lancaster from her cousin Anny Mohler of Stark County, Ohio —territory largely settled by Germans from Pennsylvania (Fig. 181). Unlike most fracturs drawn freehand or with rules and compasses, this watercolor is made from hollow-cut stencils in a variety of delightful and slightly bewildering forms. A huge rose, pinks and bellflowers in bowls, birds and a tree nearly overwhelm a standing female figure at center foreground; houses set like blocks in a row are arranged below the inscription.

While the Teutonic flavor of the fractur became Anglicized, documents and decorative pieces executed in ink and watercolor were occasionally made in New England in a manner reminiscent of Pennsylvania. A rich example, painted about 1795, is the delightful portrait of Mrs. Jacob Edwards, of Danbury, Connecticut (Fig. 182). It is a design rather than a likeness, from the painted border decorated with bellflowers, to the oversize spray of oranges, to the brightly colored and figured cotton of Mrs. Edward's gown.

A number of family records by an unknown hand come from New Hampshire. Illustrated is one with flowering vines, architectural detail and Masonic symbolism, drawn and painted to mark James Park's birth in Windham in 1795 (Fig. 183).

The idea of the illuminated manuscript continued into the nineteenth century even away from Pennsylvania. One example is a blue-outlined house, initialed E H and dated 1847, filling the space with linear design (Fig. 184). This is high-style "painting with a pen" that looks fresh and clean today.

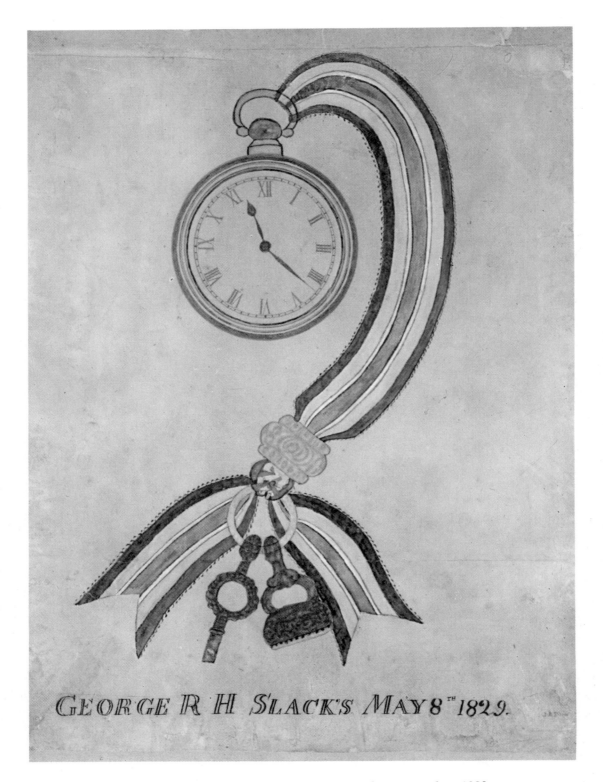

FIG. 171. J. A. TILLES. *Watch and Fob*. Watercolor, 1829.
Abby Aldrich Rockefeller Folk Art Collection

FIG. 172. Artist unknown. *Spring Blessing*. Watercolor and ink, about 1785. Museum of Fine Arts, Boston, M. and M. Karolik Collection

FIG. 173. Artist unknown. *To Herr Van Vleck, on His Birthday.* Watercolor and ink, 1795.
Moravian Historical Society

FIG. 175. Artist unknown.
Tryst on Ephrata Bridge.
Watercolor and ink, about 1810.
Collection of Martin Grossman

FIG. 174. Artist unknown. *The Prodigal Son Reveling with Harlots.* Watercolor, about 1790.
Abby Aldrich Rockefeller Folk Art Collection

FIG. 176.   JOHN VAN MINIAN. *Sarah Harley Birth Record.*
Watercolor and ink, about 1791.
Abby Aldrich Rockefeller Folk Art Collection

FIG. 177. REVEREND GEORGE GEISTWEITE. *Vorschrift.*
Watercolor and ink, 1801. Philadelphia Museum of Art

FIG. 178. Artist unknown. *Elizabeth Fedderly's New Year's Gift.* Watercolor
and ink, 1818. Collection of Martin Grossman

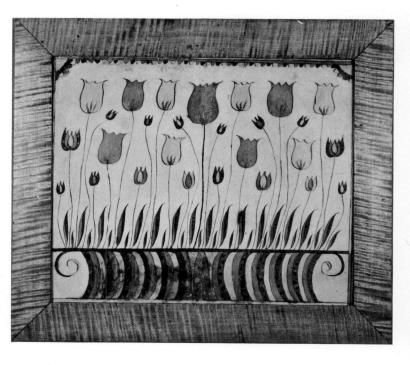

FIG. 179. Artist unknown. *Tulips in a Basket.*
Watercolor and ink, about 1810.
Henry Francis du Pont Winterthur Museum

FIG. 180. H. YOUNG. *Miss Frances Taylor.*
Watercolor and ink, 1831.
New-York Historical Society

FIG. 181. ANNY MOHLER. *Anny's Present*. Watercolor, about 1830.
Abby Aldrich Rockefeller Folk Art Collection

FIG. 182. Artist unknown. *Mrs. Jacob Edwards*. Watercolor, about 1795.
Abby Aldrich Rockefeller Folk Art Collection

FIG. 183. Artist unknown. *James Park Birth Record.*
Watercolor and ink, about 1795.
Abby Aldrich Rockefeller Folk Art Collection

FIG. 184. Artist unknown.
Blue House. Ink, 1847.
New York State Historical Association

ART INSTRUCTION FOR YOUNG LADIES

AT ITS CLOSE, the half century that began in 1800 was typified by one of its Congregational ministers as "the most remarkable the world has ever known." Young people were introduced to a society in which the three R's had not their traditional meaning but stood, instead, for republic, romanticism and religion.

In a world in which a common man thought himself a king, a quiet insurrection began to change the lot of its women. Girls and young women in areas newly civilized emerged slowly from the endless demands of pioneer life and began to seek and find education; along with their brothers they attended public schools and private academies. Women of the eighteenth century had made embroidered samplers or stitchery paintings, but this work was painstaking, eye-wracking and time-consuming. While the idea of handwork to enrich one's walls or to commemorate important events had charm, the frontier philosophy of "let's do it but let's do it quickly" led to new artistic expressions. As the century began, painting was taught in almost every female seminary, in special classes advertised far and wide by art teachers, by drawing instruction books and—eventually—by directions in magazines especially for women. Few young ladies in this era ended their study with essentials, but added the gracious art of painting in watercolor and oil.

It is only in the twentieth century that copying from sources had come to be regarded with disdain. In the centuries preceding this, artists based their work on the best inspiration they could find, Greek and Roman antiquities that had inspired artists of the Renaissance, works of leading artists of the day and, in America, at least, English mezzotints as the model for portrait, pose, costume and prop.

For schoolgirls, aids to inspiration were readily available. They came from paintings copied by their instructors; from stencils, often cut, registered and assembled into a complete design or theorem; from children's books, colored prints and Bible illustrations. Romantic compositions by the thousands remain today testifying to the work of thousands of young women.

205.

A portrait of a little girl, *Emma Clark* (Fig. 185), might be the work of an older sister or young mother. It looks like a colored copy of a woodcut from one of hundreds of children's books. The prim child in her red dress wears coral beads, a nineteenth-century charm against evil; she is seated on a hassock set on a patterned carpet. She presents her doll, who looks more like a miniature adult than the leather-bodied porcelain-headed creature that she probably was. The colors are vibrant and lively in a tiny watercolor scarcely larger than a miniature.

A ceremony at a young ladies' seminary was recorded in a romantic painting by an unknown artist (Fig. 186). Held in the open air in a grove to the right of the school building, a queen is crowned, a poem read, music played and a light collation served. One views the scene as a member of the invisible audience.

Though no schoolgirl, Mary Ann Willson is well known through a portfolio of her primitive watercolors. According to her unknown biographer, Mary Ann Willson, accompanied by another, "left their home in the East with a romantic attachment for each other" and settled in Greene County, New York. There the women bought land and built a log cabin. Her companion, Miss Brundage, farmed their few acres "by the aid of neighbors," and "occasionally did some plowing for them." Mary Ann painted naïve and vivid watercolors which she sold to neighborhood farmers. The biographer notes that the paintings were in great demand and sold as far away as Canada and "clear to Mobile." Special mention is made of Miss Willson's colors, "of the simplest kind, berries, bricks, and occasional 'store paint.'" Certainly the materials were lasting, for the colors remain brilliant to this day, vibrant in combinations reminiscent of the paint on peasant toys.

Marimaid is one of the many exotic subjects tamed to a Greene County taste and provenance (Fig. 187). The design, similar to a patchwork quilt, not only fills the paper but appears almost to burst from it in the exuberance of its style and color.

Still life was one of the most popular subjects for women, and contrasting variations on a theme illustrate the range of skill and approach. *Watermelon Slices on a Blue-Bordered Plate* is a simple and beautifully composed arrangement done—as the crisp edges of color indicate—almost entirely with stencils (Fig. 188). The blurred inner edge of plate and rind were achieved by pouncing the color onto the paper with a nearly dry bit of felt or velvet. The theme is a common one, but the stencil outlines indicate that they were made at home by the artist and did not come in a prepared theorem.

In oil, rather than watercolor, and on striped bedticking instead of paper, *Bountiful Board* presents a lively contrast to the simplicity of the watermelon slices (Fig. 189). An abundant array of fruit and nineteenth-century china, glassware and tray are arranged on a drop-leaf table laid with a checkered cloth. The table and the swagged drapery above it frame the still life effectively.

Fruit in a Glass Compote (Fig. 190), illustrates the elegant simplicity that could be achieved by using theorems. The composition is identical to another, including the sprinkling of mica flakes over the bowl to give it sparkle. But this watercolor, painted about 1820 by Emma Cady of New Lebanon, New York, demonstrates high skill in the use of stencils in contrast to its twin, which is a pedestrian effort.

Exciting forms and colors enrich a freehand still life, a large painting in oil on a wood panel, *Fruit in a Wicker Basket* (Fig. 191). Although it is copied from a print, it seems almost to spring from its space; even the corners of the board are embroidered with squiggles of paint to fill every inch.

Folk artists rarely painted realistic trompe l'oeil, preferring a warped perspective to show every facet of their subjects. Among the scarce attempts at imitation of life, few are as successful as the cat seen perched on a window ledge in front of a hatbox and beside a miscellany of pottery (Fig. 192). While the tabby seems real, fantasy reigns in a stenciled and sponged watercolor, *Bear in Tree*, that appears as a naïve and delightful arrangement (Fig. 193). Nothing is quite right in scale, but the outsize bear is providentially provided support by the twigs of a stenciled tree. A reverse of the same stencil appears at far left. Both the tiger and the antelope are made to smile in this happy scene from Texas.

A wonderful still life combining stencils and freehand drawing is nearly as innocent as *Bear in Tree;* grapes and leaves fill the space at the top of *Fruit on a Painted Tray* (Fig. 194), while the sprigged vine that rims the tray makes a rhythmic unity of the fruits assembled on it.

Romanticism, ever present in the nineteenth-century woman's mind, transports the myth of Venus, winged through the sky by her creature, the dove (in this instance, a brace of doves); the goddess is seated in a red chariot surrounded by cupids (Fig. 195). Both chariot and doves are embellished with gold-paper cutouts. The mythological scene seems quite logical as it floats on puffy clouds above a New England landscape. Trees, painted to resemble embroidery, fill the foreground. This is one of three paintings with the same subject and similar arrangement; they are probably the fulfillment of an art class assignment in a girl's school.

A conversation piece on a wood panel is a naïve and colorful copy of an illustration in a children's book. Signed once and initialed twice, *William and Mary* is the work of J. N. Eaton of Greene County (Fig. 196). Bright, clear color and design seem almost a primitive forecast of the sophisticated art of Matisse.

FIG. 185. Artist unknown. *Emma Clark.*
Watercolor, about 1810.
Abby Aldrich Rockefeller Folk Art Collection

FIG. 186. Artist unknown. *A Ceremonial at a Young Ladies' Seminary.* Oil, about 1810.
Collection of Edgar William and Bernice Chrysler Garbisch

FIG. 187. MARY ANN WILLSON. *Marimaid*. Watercolor, about 1820.
New York State Historical Association

FIG. 188. Artist unknown. *Watermelon Slices on a Blue-Bordered Plate*.
Watercolor, about 1820.
Abby Aldrich Rockefeller Folk Art Collection

FIG. 189. Artist unknown. *Bountiful Board.* Oil on bedticking, about 1855.
Abby Aldrich Rockefeller Folk Art Collection

FIG. 190. EMMA CADY. *Fruit in a Glass Compote*. Watercolor, about 1820.
Abby Aldrich Rockefeller Folk Art Collection

FIG. 191. Artist unknown. *Fruit in a Wicker Basket.* Oil on wood, about 1855.
Abby Aldrich Rockefeller Folk Art Collection

FIG. 192. Artist unknown. *Cat in Open Window.* Oil, about 1845.
Collection of Nina Fletcher Little

FIG. 193. Artist unknown. *Bear in Tree*. Watercolor, 1850.
Collection of Edgar William and Bernice Chrysler Garbisch

FIG. 194. Artist unknown. *Fruit on a Painted Tray*. Oil on velvet, about 1840.
Collection of Mrs. Holger Cahill

FIG. 195. Artist unknown. *Venus Drawn by Doves*. Watercolor on silk, about 1815. Abby Aldrich Rockefeller Folk Art Collection

FIG. 196. J. N. EATON. *William and Mary*. Oil on wood, about 1845.
Abby Aldrich Rockefeller Folk Art Collection

FOLK PAINTING FROM THE
CENTENNIAL TO YESTERDAY

Northeastern hill and valley towns provided an ideal environment in which a talented and self-taught provincial painter might flourish. These small inbred societies valued each man and woman for his or her special eccentricity or genius. In contrast, the modern world's widening and overlapping cultures make it difficult to maintain the old idea of individual worth—the idea that created a demand for the country artist's services. As the nineteenth century wore on, the ranks of self-taught provincials dwindled. Naïve artists who continued the tradition were led into the twentieth century by a handful of artisans who had begun their careers as portrait painters.

One of the leaders was Erastus Salisbury Field. By the uncommon length of his life as a working artist he became, in many ways, the most typical of the men who first prospered, and later failed through the loss of patrons. Field's last painting is not only the crowning achievement of his own career but a fitting epitaph for the legion of folk artists who once flourished in America.

In 1871, Congress authorized the 1876 Centennial Exposition to be held in Philadelphia. For Field, the coming anniversary was the occasion for a project that he had long contemplated—a historical painting that would be the climax of his career. On April 2, 1872, Field's teacher Samuel Morse died and Field's idea took on new meaning. Morse had been bitterly disappointed twice in his expectations of painting one or more of the panels in the Capitol rotunda. Following assignment of the first commission to another, Morse's friends donated two thousand dollars for a painting on a historical subject of his choice; Morse never did the work and the money was eventually returned to his patrons. A letter written to Morse in 1846 mentions the last panel for the rotunda, once more commissioned to someone else. "I hope you may yet resume the pencil, and furnish the public the most striking commentary on their utter disregard of justice by placing somewhere *The Germ of the Republic*."

The Germ of the Republic, translated from Morse to Field, became the *Historical Monument of the American Republic* completed during the first half of the centennial year (Fig. 197). Although it was a different conception from Morse's—Field was as violently against slavery as Morse was for it—disappointment over the lack of interest in his work beyond the confines of his home town, was as bitter for Field as a similar rejection had been for his teacher.

Field's patron for the last thirty years of his life was his much younger third cousin Stephen Ashley Hubbard, the managing editor of the *Hartford Courant*. In March, 1872, General Joseph R. Hawley, the publisher of the *Courant*, became president of the United States Centennial Commission for the fair at Philadelphia. To Field this must have seemed a gift from the angels, for Hawley was Stephen Hubbard's patron just as Hubbard was his. Field undoubtedly knew the head of the centennial commission. If he did not, he would certainly have counted on his cousin to forward his interests.

To modern eyes the painting is superior in every way to the typical genre scenes of Turkish slaves and homely country incidents that were shown at Philadelphia. But the *Monument* was never on view at the Centennial. If it appeared at all it was in Edward Bierstadt's fine small "photoplate print" and not as the great and final achievement of Erastus Field's life. The painting is history in the grand manner. Towers in different architectural styles spring high in the air from a long base that almost fills the fourteen-foot width of the canvas. Every level of each tower is keyed to an incident in American history and illustrated in grisaille as bas-relief or sculpture in the round. In the highest rooms Field envisioned exhibitions illustrating American life. His crowning image is an aerial railway with balloon-stack engines that connects the exhibition rooms of the seven original towers. The *Monument* was a grand and extraordinary composition that astounded neighbors, friends and relations. There was nothing in or out of the Connecticut Valley to equal it, and visitors came to the red-painted Hubbard barn, across the road from Field's small house in Plumtrees, to watch, encourage and commend the project. Despite the fancifulness of the magic *Monument*, Yankee farmers admired the artist's work and respected his vocation, though it was decidedly different from the usual ones in Leverett and Plumtrees.

Even as the camera snatched commissions away from the nineteenth-century folk artist, he turned to other themes. The primitive painter of the contemporary world rarely chooses the portrait as his subject. Most often, he unknowingly reviews all the other subjects that inspired earlier artists. He captures the unusual happenings of his town, the landscape he sees, the religion he believes and the history he respects.

217.

From the centennial anniversary of independence to yesterday, the few who preserve the tradition of the folk artist in America are most often self-taught men and women who have always lived in societies isolated by geographic, economic or ethnic considerations. Isolation from the modern world seems almost necessary for the development of the primitive artist who finds individual solutions to artistic problems.

Pennsylvania almshouses provided just such isolation for three men in the latter part of the nineteenth century who created vivid portraits of the state's poorhouses. Both the Bucks and Berks County almshouses exist in several painted versions, but only one portrait of the Montgomery County almshouse is known (Fig. 199). The view is a fascinating one, rich in detail. The artist, Charles Hofmann, was an inmate of several institutions in the 1870s "via the alcohol route." It is tempting to identify one of the two figures seated at right foreground as the artist; both are shown fishing as a bottle is passed between them. The county farm's immaculately cultivated fields and orchards are illustrated. Resisting the impulse to reflect the entire scene in a flipped mirror image in the waters of the Schuylkill, the artist shows only the green-painted walls and blue roof of the almshouse; by using this device, the two barges that move along the river effectively balance the lower third of the richly-colored composition.

On July 2, 1881, President Garfield was assassinated. Erastus Field promptly turned out several miniature bust portraits on academy board of the murdered president and went from house to house in Leverett and Sunderland attempting to sell them for a dollar apiece. Times had indeed changed.

While New Englanders rejected the artist they had once welcomed, the West opened to the naïve painter. The same year that Field was hawking his pictures in central Massachusetts, the *Residence of Mr E. R. Jones* was portrayed in watercolor by Paul Seifert in Dodgeville, Wisconsin (Fig. 198). The winter scene from the Midwest places emphasis on the chief features of the farm landscape in which trees and fences impose a precise order. The artist was born in Dresden, Germany, and came to America after the Civil War; he worked as a taxidermist also. His farmscapes are painted on colored papers, a device that permitted him to use color in an original way to highlight and shade the median hue of his backgrounds. Fine composition and precisionist detail distinguish his delightfully fresh, large watercolors.

The sentimental Victorian tradition of nostalgic memories recalled in old age was most notably continued into twentieth-century folk art by Anna Maria Robertson Moses (Fig. 200). The fabled Grandma Moses became, in the eyes of many Americans, the symbol of a folk artist. The aged painter remained active in her late-blooming profession until shortly before her death at the age of 101.

But Grandma Moses was neither the best nor the last of the painters who followed the folk tradition. In Marblehead, Massachusetts, an old retired fisherman raised seeds and flowers and sold them door to door. About 1920, J. O. J. Frost taught himself to paint. He carved and polychromed several fish as a reminder of his former trade and began a historical series depicting scenes from Marblehead's long and illustrious history (Figs. 201, 203). The drawing and colors are childlike but the incidents of Marblehead's daily life are not only fresh and uninhibited but accurate and dramatic records as well.

In contrast to the innocent charm of Grandma Moses and J. O. J. Frost is the raw power of John Kane. A Pittsburgh steelworker, Kane found means for esthetic self-expression in a stylized, precisionist portrait of himself and his environment. His self-portrait is a masterpiece (Fig. 202); a sinewy, tense, symmetrical figure is set like a carved icon within a painted arch. Only incidentally does the viewer see that the design of the arch appears as three bent steel bars.

Kane's paintings of *Turtle Creek Valley* are powerful, strong views of an industrial city (Fig. 204). In contrast, another modern composition of a similar subject is delicate, light and airy. *The Day The Bosque Froze Over* by Clara McDonald Williamson (Fig. 205), was painted in 1953; except for the costumes one would not have been surprised if it had been dated 1853.

One of the most entertaining portraits in the folk tradition is *Tinkle, A Cat* (Fig. 206). Not only is the cat's name recorded, but his age as well. He was two years old in 1883 when the portrait was painted. While the name and age of the subject are known, the artist is not. The tradition of the anonymous artist continues long past its prime. Another late folk artist was inspired by the New Jersey winter landscape. *Echo Rock* is an almost surrealistic scene (Fig. 207). A large stag appears in the foreground, the pattern of his antlers endlessly repeated in a receding forest of bare-branched trees. Civilization intrudes in the form of a harnessed team and wild nature is represented by an owl on a tree limb.

Selective realism is used to express the beauty of untouched nature in *Wallowa Lake* painted in 1927 by Steve Harley of Michigan (Fig. 208). The painting represents one-third of Harley's major works, and is signed by him "S. W. Harley (The Invincible)." It is a painted record of a country that he first saw after he was fifty. Dissatisfied with photographs, he painted three scenes from life, aiding his memory as the seasons changed with snapshots and sketches. Steve Harley returned to Michigan after years in the northwest and spent the last decade of his life in a tiny, ramshackle cabin. Daylight entered through the door and a single window; the room glowed with the reflected light of Harley's three remarkable paintings.

Exotic rather than real nature inspired the retired manufacturer of women's clothes, Morris Hirshfield. *Tiger* (Fig. 209), completed in 1940, is an exciting design study in which the creature's stripes are repeated in a sky that seems almost in flames. Tidy trees, plants and textured mountains tie the composition to earth.

In his old age, Olaf Krans painted memoirs of his childhood at Bishop Hill, a Swedish religious colony in Illinois. Among the few portraits by twentieth-century folk artists is the painting of his mother, *Mrs. Eric Krans,* which dates to about 1900 (Fig. 210). In spite of distinctive facial features, a printed linoleum rug on the floor, a wallpaper border and a ribboned vase of flowers—all in turn of the century country style—the study is strongly reminiscent of Whistler's famous portrait of his mother, *Arrangement in Grey and Black*.

Among the most recent folk paintings is *Benediction* by Harriet French Turner of Roanoke (Fig. 211) illustrating a Dunkard meeting in western Virginia. The colors are clear and true and the painting is careful and painstaking. The Dunkards are seen from a high vantage point so that the devout figures are sharply etched against a dark floor rather than pale walls.

A Pennsylvanian, Joseph Pickett, produced only a handful of paintings, all based on the state's history and landscape. *Washington Under the Council Tree* (Fig. 212), painted about 1910, shows the familiar equestrian figure beneath the branches of a tree painted with impasto so thick it seems encrusted with history and age.

A similar device is used by the Negro painter Horace Pippin of West Chester, Pennsylvania, in his *Domino Players*, about 1935 (Fig. 213). Contrasting light dresses against dark woodwork and dark heads against white-washed walls, he creates a dynamic pattern that illustrates a domestic scene. Pippin's *Peaceable Kingdom* was inspired by those of Edward Hicks (Fig. 214), but Pippin's version is a free, naturalistic view in contrast to Hicks's intentional symbolism and controlled design.

As history inspired earlier members of the self-taught fraternity of artists, it continued in its appeal to modern members. In *John Brown Going to His Hanging* (Fig. 215), Horace Pippin found a subject close to his interest and sympathy. The scene is powerful in its simplicity. It is almost monochromatic, outlined in earth tones balanced with areas of black and white. The dark prison bars and the strong outlines of trees nearly bare stand out against a light background; they form an effective contrast to the dark bodies massed in the foreground. John Brown's solid, bound figure is engraved against white in the center of the painting.

The closing years of the long history of the folk artist in America are quieter and far less exhilarating than the beginning. The portrait of the artist who taught himself and found individual solutions to problems in order to create provincial works of art remains in his works. But the need to paint in this way and the naïve means for fulfilling the need have almost ceased to exist in a sophisticated and nonindividualistic culture. But the best of the flood of art works by these bold, inventive and imaginative men and women continue to intrigue and delight a different world and society.

FIG. 197. ERASTUS SALISBURY FIELD.
Historical Monument of the American Republic.
Oil on canvas, 1873—1876, with later additions.
Museum of Fine Arts, Springfield, Massachusetts,
Morgan Wesson Memorial Collection

HISTORICAL MONUMENT OF THE AMERICAN REPUBLIC.

Residence of Mr E. R. Jones. Town Dodgeville. Wis. 1881.

FIG. 199. CHARLES HOFMANN. *View of the Montgomery County Almshouse Buildings.* Oil, 1878.
Abby Aldrich Rockefeller Folk Art Collection

FIG. 198. PAUL SEIFERT. *Residence of Mr E. R. Jones.* Watercolor, 1881.
New York State Historical Association

FIG. 200. ANNA MARIA ROBERTSON MOSES. *Catching the Turkey*. Oil, 1943.
Galerie St. Etienne
Collection of Henry S. McNeil

FIG. 201. J. O. J. FROST. *There Shall Be No More War*. Oil, about 1920.
Collection of Nina Fletcher Little

FIG. 202. JOHN KANE.
Self-Portrait. Oil, 1929. Museum of Modern Art,
Abby Aldrich Rockefeller Fund

FIG. 203. J. O. J. FROST. *Marblehead Harbor*. Oil, about 1925.
Marblehead Historical Society

FIG. 204.   JOHN KANE. *Turtle Creek Valley No. 1*. Oil, 1927. Terry De Lapp Gallery

FIG. 205.   CLARA WILLIAMSON. *The Day The Bosque Froze Over*. Oil, 1953. Museum of Modern Art

FIG. 206. Artist unknown.
Tinkle, A Cat.
Oil, 1883.
Shelburne Museum

FIG. 207. Artist unknown.
Echo Rock.
Oil, about 1890.
Collection of Herbert W. Hemphill, Jr.

FIG. 208. STEVE HARLEY. *Wallowa Lake*. Oil, 1927. Abby Aldrich Rockefeller Folk Art Collection

FIG. 209. MORRIS HIRSHFIELD. *Tiger*. Oil, 1940. Museum of Modern Art, Abby Aldrich Rockefeller Fund

FIG. 210. OLAF KRANS. *Mrs. Eric Krans.* Oil, about 1900.
Chicago Historical Society

FIG. 211. HARRIET FRENCH TURNER.
Benediction. Oil, 1963.
Abby Aldrich Rockefeller
Folk Art Collection

FIG. 212. **JOSEPH PICKETT.** *Washington Under the Council Tree.*
Oil, about 1910.   Newark Museum

FIG. 213. **HORACE PIPPIN.** *Domino Players.* Oil, about 1935.
Phillips Collection

FIG. 214. HORACE PIPPIN. *Peaceable Kingdom*. Oil, 1944.
Encyclopaedia Britannica Collection

FIG. 215. **HORACE PIPPIN.** *John Brown Going to His Hanging.* Oil, c. 1930.
Pennsylvania Academy of the Fine Arts

BIBLIOGRAPHY

BOOKS

A

Allen, Edward B. *Early American Wall Paintings, 1710–1850*. New Haven: 1926.

Andrews, Edward D. *The People Called Shakers*. Second edition. New York: Dover Publications, Inc., 1963.

B

Barker, Virgil. *American Painting, History and Interpretation*. New York: The Macmillan Company, 1950.

Bayley, Frank W., and Charles E. Goodspeed, editors; William Dunlap, author. *A History of the Rise and Progress of the Arts of Design in the United States*. New edition, 3 Vols. Boston: C. E. Goodspeed, 1918.

Belknap, Henry W. *Artists and Craftsmen of Essex County, Mass*. Salem: Essex Institute, 1927.

Belknap, Waldron Phoenix, Jr. *American Painting, Materials for a History*. Cambridge, Massachusetts: The Belknap Press of the Harvard University Press, 1959.

Bolton, Theodore, and Irwin F. Cortelyou. *Ezra Ames of Albany, Portrait Painter, Craftsman, Royal Arch Mason, Banker, 1768–1836, and a Catalogue of his Works* by Irwin F. Cortelyou. New York: The New-York Historical Society, 1955.

Born, Wolfgang. *American Landscape Painting; An Interpretation*. New Haven: Yale University Press, 1948.

———. *Still-Life Painting in America*. New York: Oxford University Press, 1947.

Brown, Ralph Hall. *Mirror for Americans; Likeness of the Eastern Seaboard, 1810*. New York: American Geographical Society, 1943.

Burroughs, Alan. *John Greenwood in America, 1745–1752*. Andover, Massachusetts: Addison Gallery of American Art, Phillips Academy, 1943.

———. *Limners and Likenesses; Three Centuries of American Painting*. Cambridge, Massachusetts: Harvard University Press, 1936.

Butts, Porter. *Art in Wisconsin*. Madison: Democrat Printing Co., 1936.

C

Cahill, Holger. *American Folk Art, the Art of The Common Man in America 1750–1900*. New York: W. W. Norton & Co. Inc., 1932.

Catesby, Mark. *The Natural History of Carolina, Florida and the Bahama Islands*. London: Printed for C. Marsh, 1754.

Chase, Mary Ellen. *Jonathan Fisher, Maine Parson, 1768–1847*. New York: The Macmillan Company, 1948.

Craig, James H. *The Arts and Crafts in North Carolina 1699–1840*. Winston-Salem, North Carolina: Museum of Early Southern Decorative Arts, 1966.

D

Davenport, Millia. *The Book of Costume*. 2 Vols. New York: Crown Publishers, Inc., 1948.

Davidson, Marshall. *Life in America*. 2 Vols. Boston: Houghton Mifflin Company, 1951.

Dow, George F. *The Arts and Crafts in Early New England*. Topsfield, Massachusetts: The Wayside Press, 1927.

Drepperd, Carl W. *American Drawing Books*. New York: The New York Public Library, 1946.

———. *American Pioneer Arts and Artists*. Springfield, Massachusetts: Pond-Ekberg Co., 1942.

Dresser, Louisa. *XVIIth Century Painting in New England . . .* Worcester, Massachusetts: Worcester Art Museum, 1935.

Dunlap, William. *A History of the Rise and Progress of the Arts of Design in the United States*, 2 Vols. New York: George P. Scott and Co., 1834.

E

Eberlein, Harold D., and Abbot McClure. *The Practical Book of Early American Arts and Crafts*. Philadelphia and London: J. B. Lippincott Company, 1916.

F

Fielding, Mantle. *Dictionary of American Painters, Sculptors, and Engravers*. [Philadelphia, printed for the subscribers, 1926.] 3rd ed. New York: J. F. Carr, 1965.

Flexner, James Thomas. *America's Old Masters; First Artists of the New World*. New York: The Viking Press, Inc., 1939.

———. *First Flowers of Our Wilderness, American Painting*. Boston: Houghton Mifflin Company, 1947.

———. *The Light of Distant Skies, 1760–1835*. New York: Harcourt, Brace and Co., 1954.

Ford, Alice. *Edward Hicks, Painter of The Peaceable Kingdom*. Philadelphia: University of Pennsylvania Press, 1952.

———. *Pictorial Folk Art New England to California*. New York and London: The Studio Publications, Inc., 1949.

Frankenstein, Alfred. *After the Hunt: William Harnett and Other American Still Life Painters, 1870–1900*. Berkeley and Los Angeles: University of California Press, 1953.

French, Henry W. *Art and Artists in Connecticut*. Boston: Lee and Shepard, 1879.

G

Gardner, Albert T. E. *101 Masterpieces of American Primitive Painting* from the Collection of Edgar

William and Bernice Chrysler Garbish. New Ed., New York: Doubleday and Company, Inc., 1962.

———, and Stuart Feld. *American Paintings, a Catalogue of the Collection of The Metropolitan Museum of Art*. New York: The Metropolitan Museum of Art, 1965.

Gottesman, Rita S. *The Arts and Crafts in New York 1726–1776*. New York: The New-York Historical Society, 1937.

———. *The Arts and Crafts in New York 1777–1799*. New York: The New-York Historical Society, 1954.

———. *The Arts and Crafts in New York 1800–1804*. New York: The New-York Historical Society, 1966.

Groce, George C., and David H. Wallace. *The New-York Historical Society's Dictionary of Artists in America 1564–1860*. New Haven: Yale University Press, 1957.

H

Hagen, Oskar. *The Birth of the American Tradition of Art*. New York: Charles Scribner's Sons, 1940.

Hicks, Edward. *Memoirs of the Life and Religious Labors of Edward Hicks* . . . Philadelphia: Merrihew and Thompson, Printers, 1851.

J

Janis, Sidney. *They Taught Themselves; American Primitive Painters of the Twentieth Century*. Foreword by Alfred H. Barr, Jr. New York: Dial Press, 1942.

K

Kauffman, Henry. *Pennsylvania Dutch American Folk Art*. New York and London: Studio Publications, 1946.

L

Larkin, Oliver W. *Art and Life in America*. New York: Rinehart & Co., Inc., 1949.

———. *Samuel F. B. Morse and American Democratic Art*. Boston and Toronto: Little, Brown and Company, 1954.

Lichten, Frances. *Folk Art Motifs of Pennsylvania*. New York: Hastings House, 1954.

———. *Folk Art of Rural Pennsyl-* *vania*. New York: Charles Scribner's Sons, 1946.

Lipman, Jean. *American Primitive Painting*. New York: Oxford University Press, 1942.

———, ed. *What Is American in American Art*. New York: McGraw-Hill Book Co., Inc., 1963.

———, and Eve Meulendyke. *American Folk Decoration*. New York: Oxford University Press, 1951.

———, and Alice Winchester, eds. *Primitive Painters in America 1750–1950, an anthology*. New York: Dodd, Mead & Co., 1950.

Little, Nina Fletcher. *American Decorative Wall Painting 1700–1850*. Sturbridge, Massachusetts: Old Sturbridge Village, 1952.

———. *The Abby Aldrich Rockefeller Folk Art Collection, A Descriptive Catalogue*. Boston: Little Brown & Co., 1957.

London, Hannah R. *Portraits of Jews by Gilbert Stuart and Other Early American Artists*. New York: 1927.

Lorant, Stefan. *The New World; The First Pictures of America, Made by John White and Jacques Le Moyne and Engraved by Theodore De Bry* . . . New York: Duell, Sloan & Pearce, Inc., 1946.

M

M. and M. Karolik Collection of American Paintings 1815–1865. 2 Vols. Boston: Museum of Fine Arts, 1949.

Miller, Perry. *The Life of the Mind in America from the Revolution to the Civil War*. New York: Harcourt, Brace & World, Inc., 1965.

Morse, Edward L. *Samuel F. B. Morse, His Letters and Journals*. 2 Vols. Boston and New York: Houghton Mifflin Company, 1914.

Moses, Anna. *Grandma Moses; My Life's History*, edited by Otto Kallir. New York: Harper & Brothers, 1952.

N

New York City Directories

Noble, Louis Legrand. *The Life and Works of Thomas Cole*. Cambridge, Massachusetts: The Belknap Press of Harvard University Press, 1964.

P

Peat, Wilbur D. *Pioneer Painters of Indiana*. Indianapolis: Art Association of Indianapolis, 1954.

Peters, Harry T. *America on Stone*. Garden City, New York: Doubleday, Doran and Co., Inc., 1931.

Pierce, Frederick Clifton. *Field Genealogy*. 2 Vols. Chicago: Hammond Press, W. B. Conkey Co., 1901.

Pierson, William H., and Martha Davidson. *Arts of the United States, a Pictorial Survey*. New York: McGraw Hill Book Co., Inc., 1960.

Porter, Rufus. *A Select Collection of Valuable and Curious Arts*. 2nd edition. Concord, New Hampshire: 1826.

Prime, Alfred Coxe. *The Arts and Crafts in Philadelphia, Maryland and South Carolina 1721–1785*. Topsfield, Massachusetts: The Walpole Society, 1929.

———. *The Arts and Crafts in Philadelphia, Maryland and South Carolina 1786–1800*. Topsfield, Massachusetts: The Walpole Society, 1932.

Prowell, George R. *Beers History of York County, Pennsylvania*. Chicago: J. H. Beers & Co., 1907.

R

Reichel, William C. *History of the Rise, Progress, and Present Condition of the Moravian Seminary for Young Ladies at Bethlehem, Pa.*, 2d ed. Philadelphia: 1874.

Richardson, Edgar P. *American Romantic Painting*. New York: E. Weyhe, 1944.

———. *Painting in America. The Story of 450 Years*. New York: Thomas Y. Crowell Company, 1956.

[Rossiter, Henry]. *M & M Karolik Collection of American Watercolors and Drawings 1800–1875*. 2 Vols. Boston: Museum of Fine Arts, 1962.

Runk, Emma Ten Broeck. *The Ten Broeck Genealogy* . . . New York: The De Vinne Press, 1897.

Rutledge, Anna Wells. *Artists in the Life of Charleston, through Colony and State from Restoration to Reconstruction*. Philadelphia: American Philosophical Society (*Transactions*, Vol. XXXIX, Part 2), 1949.

———. *Cumulative Record of Exhibition Catalogues, The Pennsylvania Academy of the Fine Arts, 1807–1870, the Society of Artists, 1800–1814, the Artists' Fund Society, 1835–1845.* Philadelphia: American Philosophical Society (*Transactions,* Vol. XXXVIII), 1955.

S

Sears, Clara Endicott. *Some American Primitives.* Boston: Houghton Mifflin Company, 1941.

Shelley, Donald A. *A Catalogue of American Portraits in The New-York Historical Society.* New York: The New-York Historical Society, 1941.

———. *The Fraktur-Writings or Illuminated Manuscripts of the Pennsylvania Germans.* Allentown, Pennsylvania: The Pennsylvania German Folklore Society, 1961.

Sherman, Frederic F. *Early American Painting.* New York and London: The Century Company, 1932.

———. *Richard Jennys, New England Portrait Painter.* Springfield, Massachusetts: Pond-Ekberg Company, 1941.

Smith, G. M. *History of the Town of Sunderland, Massachusetts.* Greenfield, Massachusetts: E. A. Hall and Co., 1899.

Stoudt, John J. *Early Pennsylvania Arts and Crafts.* New York and London: A. S. Barnes & Co., 1964.

———. *Pennsylvania Folk Art.* Allentown, Pennsylvania: The Pennsylvania German Folklore Society, 1948.

T

Trollope, Frances M. *Domestic Manners of the Americans.* London: Whittaker, Treacher and Company, 1832.

V

Vanderpoel, Emily N. *Chronicles of a Pioneer School.* 2 Vols. Cambridge, Massachusetts: University Press, 1903.

W

Waring, Janet. *Early American Wall Stencils. Their Origin, History and Use . . .* New York: William R. Scott, Inc., 1937.

Weddell, Alexander, W. (ed.), *Virginia Historical Portraiture, 1585–1830,* Richmond: The William Byrd Press, Inc., 1930.

Wright, Richardson. *Hawkers and Walkers in Early America.* Philadelphia: J. B. Lippincott Co., 1927.

PERIODICALS

A

Allen, E. B. "The Quaint Frescoes of New England," *Art in America,* Vol. IX, No. 6 (1922), 263–274.

Allen, O. P. "Painter of Portraits," *Palmer Journal* (May 22, 1913).

"American Primitive Painting: Collection of Edgar William and Bernice Chrysler Garbisch," *Art in America,* Vol. XLII, No. 2 (1954), 94–166.

B

Barker, Virgil. "Colloquial History Painting," *Art in America,* Vol. XLII, No. 2 (1964) 118–125, 156.

———. "Native Painting—a Revolution," *Art in America,* Vol. XL, No. 1 (1952), 21–28.

Baur, John I. H. "Unknown American Painters of the 19th Century," *College Art Journal,* Vol. VI (Summer, 1947), 277–282.

Black, Mary C. "American Primitive Watercolors," *Art in America,* Vol. LI, No. 4 (1963), 64–82.

———. "The Case of the Red and Green Birds," *Arts in Virginia,* Vol. III, No. 2 (Winter, 1963), 2–9.

———. "Erastus Salisbury Field," *Art in America,* Vol. LI, No. 1 (1963), 82–83.

———. "Erastus Salisbury Field," *Art in America,* Vol. LIV, No. 1 (1966), 49–56.

———. "Erastus Salisbury Field and the Sources of his Inspiration," *Antiques,* Vol. LXXXIII, No. 2 (February, 1963), 201 ff.

———. "A Folk Art Whodunit," *Art in America,* Vol. LIII, No. 3 (1965), 96–105.

———. "A Little Child Shall Lead Them," *Arts in Virginia,* Vol. I, No. 1 (Fall, 1960), 22–29.

——— and Stuart Feld. "John Bradley From Great Britton," *Antiques,* Vol. XC, No. 4 (October, 1966).

Born, Wolfgang. "Notes on Still Life Painting in America," *Antiques,* Vol. L, No. 3 (September, 1946), 158–160.

Brown, W. R. "Painter Field," editorial, *The Amherst Record* (June, 1947).

Bushnell, David I., Jr. "John White: The First English Artist to Visit America, 1585," *The Virginia Magazine,* Vol. XXXV (October, 1927), 419–30; Vol. XXXVI (January, 1928), 17–26 (April, 1928), 124–134.

Bye, Arthur Edwin. "Edward Hicks," *Art in America,* Vol. XXXIX, No. 1 (February, 1951), 25–35.

———. "Edward Hicks, Painter-Preacher," *Antiques,* Vol. XXIX, No. 1 (January, 1936), 13–16.

C

Cahill, Holger. "American Folk Art," *American Collector,* Vol. IV, No. 11 (November 14, 1935), 3.

———. "American Folk Art," *American Mercury,* Vol. XXIV (September, 1931), 39–46.

———. "Artisan and Amateur in American Folk Art," *Antiques,* Vol. LIX, No. 3 (March, 1951), 210–211.

———. "Folk Art, Its Place in the American Tradition," *Parnassus,* Vol. IV (March, 1932), 39–46.

Chamson, André, translated by Elinor Merrell. "Physiognotrace Profiles," *Antiques,* Vol. IX, No. 3 (March, 1926), 147–149.

Christensen, Irwin O. "An American Primitive Portrait Group," *Antiques,* Vol. LXXI, No. 6 (June, 1957), 541.

Comstock, Helen. "An 18th Century Audubon," *Antiques,* Vol. XXXVII, No. 6 (June, 1940), 282–284.

———. "Portraits of American Craftsmen," *Antiques,* Vol. LXXIII, No. 4 (October, 1959), 320–323.

Cortelyou, Irwin F. "Henry Conover: Sitter, Not Artist," *Antiques,* Vol. LXVI, No. 6 (December, 1954), 481.

———. "Micah Williams, Pastellist," *Antiques,* Vol. LIXXX, No. 5 (November, 1960), 459–461.

———. "A Mysterious Pastellist Identified," *Antiques,* Vol. LXVI (August, 1954), 122–124.

———. "Notes on Micah Williams, Native of New Jersey," *Antiques,*

LXII, No. 6 (December, 1958), 540–541.

Cowles, Fleur. "H. O. Kelly's 'Penning Goats'," *Art in America*, Vol. XLVI, No. 3 (1958), 50–51.

D

Dods, Agnes M. "A Check List of Portraits and Paintings by Erastus Salisbury Field," *Art in America*, Vol. XXXII, No. 1 (1944), 32–40.

———. "Erastus Salisbury Field (1805–1900) A New England Folk Artist," *Old-Time New England*, Vol. XXXIII (October, 1942), 26–32.

———. "More About Jennys," *Art in America*, Vol. XXXIV, No. 2 (1946), 114–116.

———. "Nathan and Joseph Negus, itinerant painters," *Antiques*, Vol. LXIII, No. 5 (November, 1959), 434–437.

———. "Newly Discovered Portraits by J. William Jennys," *Art in America*, Vol. XXXIII, No. 1 (1945), 4–12.

Drepperd, Carl W. "American Drawing Books," *New York Public Library Bulletin*, Vol. XLIX (November, 1945), 795–812.

———. "Art Instruction Books for the People," *Antiques*, Vol. XLI, No. 6 (June, 1942), 356–359.

———. "Early American Advertising Art," New York City: Paul A. Struck, 1945.

———. "Still Life and Pretty Pieces," *Art in America*, Vol. XLII, No. 2 (1964), 126–134.

E

Eckhardt, George H. "The Henry S. Borneman Collection of Pennsylvania-German Fracturs," *Antiques*, Vol. LXXI, No. 6 (June, 1957), 538–540.

F

Flexner, James Thomas. "The Amazing William Williams: Painter, Author, Teacher, Musician, State Designer, Castaway," *Magazine of Art*, Vol. XXXVII (November, 1944), 242–246, 276–278.

———. "The Art of the Primitives," *American Heritage*, Vol. VII, No. 2 (February, 1955), 38–47.

———. "Inhabited Landscapes," *Art in America*, Vol. XLII, No. 2 (1964), 106–111.

———. "Pieter Vanderlyn, Come Home," *Antiques*, Vol. LXXIII, No. 6 (June, 1959), 546–549.

———. "Winthrop Chandler: An 18th-Century Artisan Painter," *Magazine of Art*, Vol. XL (November, 1947), 274–278.

Ford, Alice. "The Publication of Edward Hicks's Memoirs," *Bulletin of Friends Historical Association*, Vol. L, No. 1 (Spring, 1961), 4–11.

Frankenstein, Alfred and Healy, Arthur K. D. "Two Journeyman Painters, Benjamin Franklin Mason and Abraham G. D. Tuthill," *Art in America*, Vol. XXXVIII, No. 1 (1950), 3–63.

Fraser, Esther Stevens. "Some Colonial and Early American Decorative Floors," *Antiques*, Vol. XIX, No. 4 (April, 1931), 296–301.

G

Gardner, Albert Ten Eyck. "New Names in American Art," *Art in America*, Vol. XLVIX, No. 4 (1961), 80–83.

———. "An Old New York Family," *Art in America*, Vol. LI, No. 3 (1963), 58–61.

Groce, George C. "New York Painting before 1800," *New York History*, Vol. XIX (January, 1938), 44–57.

———. "Who Was J[ohn?] Cooper," *Art Quarterly*, Vol. XVIII (Spring, 1955), 73–82.

H

Hacker, Inge. "Discovery of a Prodigy," *Museum of Fine Arts [Boston] Bulletin*, Vol. LXI, No. 323, 23–29.

Halpert, Edith Gregor. "In Memoriam," *Art in America*, Vol. XLII, No. 2 (1964), 135–138, 158–162.

Hastings, Mrs. Russell. "Pieter Vanderlyn, a Hudson River Portrait Painter (1687 – 1778)," *Antiques*, Vol. XLII, No. 6 (December, 1942), 296–299.

Held, Julius S. "Edward Hicks and the Tradition," *Art Quarterly*, Vol. XIV [Summer, 1951], 121–136.

Holdridge, Barbara and Lawrence. "Ammi Phillips," *Art in America*, Vol. XLVIII, No. 2 (1960), 98–103.

———. "Ammi Phillips, Limner Ex-traordinary," *Antiques*, Vol. LXXX, No. 6 [December, 1961], 558–563.

Howland, Garth A. "John Valentine Haidt, a Little Known 18th Century Painter," *Pennsylvania History*, Vol. VIII, No. 11 (October, 1941), 304–313.

J

Jackson, Joseph. "Krimmel, 'The American Hogarth,'" *International Studio*, Vol. XCIII (June, 1929), 33–36, 86, 88.

Jones, Agnes Halsey. "New-Found Art of the Young Republic," *Antiques*, Vol. LIXXX, No. 1 (July, 1960), 64–65.

———. "Rediscovered Paintings of Upstate New York," *Art in America*, Vol. XLVI, No. 2 (1958), 74–77.

Jones, Louis C. "Daily Life of the American Folk," *Art in America*, Vol. XLII, No. 2 (1964), 112–117, 158.

———. "The Folk Art Collection, Fenimore House, Cooperstown," *Art in America*, Vol. XXXVIII, No. 2 (April, 1950), 109–127.

———. "Liberty and Considerable License," *Antiques*, Vol. LXXII, No. 1 (July, 1958), 558–559.

———, and Marshall B. Davidson. "American Folk Art in Fenimore House, Cooperstown, N. Y." The Metropolitan Museum of Art Miniatures, Album LZ (1953).

K

Karr, Louise. "Paintings on Velvet," *Antiques*, Vol. XX, No. 3 (September, 1931), 162–165.

Kellner, Sydney. "The Beginnings of Landscape Painting in America," *Art in America*, Vol. XXVI (October, 1938), 158–168.

L

Lipman, Jean. "Amateur Art: An American Tradition," *Art News*, Vol. LI, No. 9 (January, 1952), 8, 60.

———. "American Primitive Portraiture—a Revaluation," *Antiques*, Vol. XL, No. 3 (September, 1941), 142–144.

———. "American Townscapes," *Antiques*, Vol. XLVI, No. 6 (December, 1944), 340–341.

———. "Asahel Powers, Painter," *Antiques,* Vol. LXXIII, No. 6 (June, 1959), 558–559.

———. "Benjamin Greenleaf, New England Limner," *Antiques,* Vol. LII, No. 3 (September, 1947), 195–197.

———. "Collecting American Primitives," *American Collector,* Vol. XI, No. 9 (October, 1942), 10–11, 17.

———. "The Composite Scene in Primitive Painting," *Gazette des Beaux-Arts,* (February, 1946), 119–128.

———. "A Critical Definition of the American Primitive," *Art in America,* Vol. XXVI, No. 4 (1938), 171–177.

———. "Deborah Goldsmith, Itinerant Portrait Painter," *Antiques,* Vol. XLIV, No. 5 (November, 1943), 227–229.

———. "Eunice Pinney, An Early Connecticut Water-colorist," *Art Quarterly,* Vol. VI (Summer, 1943), 213–221.

———. "I. J. H. Bradley, Portrait Painter," *Art in America,* Vol. XXXIII (July, 1945), 154–166.

———. "James Sanford Ellsworth—a Postscript," *Art in America,* Vol. XXXII, No. 2 (1944), 101–102.

———. "Joseph H. Hidley (1830–1872): His New York Townscapes," *American Collector,* Vol. XVI (June, 1947), 10–11.

———. "Mermaids in Folk Art," *Antiques,* Vol. LIII, No. 3 (March, 1948), 211–213.

———. "Miss Willson's Watercolors," *American Collector,* Vol. XIII (February, 1944), 8–9, 20.

[Lipman, Jean.] "The Peaceable Kingdom by Three Pennsylvania Primitives," *Art in America,* Vol. XLV, No. 3 (1957), 28–29.

———. "Points About Primitives." *American Collector,* Vol. 15, No. 2 (March, 1946), 8–9.

———. "Primitive Vision and Modern Design," *Art in America,* Vol. XXXII, No. 1 (1944), 11–19.

———. "Print to Primitive," *Antiques,* Vol. LX, No. 1 (July, 1946), 41–43.

———. "Rufus Porter, Yankee Wall Painter," *Art in America,* Vol. XXXVIII, No. 3 [1950], 132–200.

———. "The Study of Folk Art," *Art in America,* Vol. XXXIII, No. 4 (1945), 245–254.

Little, Nina Fletcher. "Coach, Sign and Fancy Painting," *Art in America,* Vol. XLII, No. 2 (1964), 147–152, 166.

———. "Doctor Rufus Hathaway, Physician and Painter of Duxbury, Massachusetts, 1770–1822," *Art in America,* Vol. XLI, No. 3 (Summer, 1953), 95–139.

———. "Earliest Signed Picture by T. Chambers . . . ," *Antiques,* Vol. LIII, No. 4 (April, 1948), 285.

———. "Itinerant Painting in America, 1750–1850," *New York History,* Vol. XXX (April, 1949), 204–216.

———. "J. O. J. Frost," *Art in America,* Vol. XLIII, No. 3 (1955), 28–33.

———. "John Brewster Jr., 1766–1854, Deaf-mute Itinerant Portrait Painter," *Antiques,* Vol. LIXXX, No. 5 (November, 1960), 462–463.

———. "Little-Known Connecticut Limners," *Art in America,* Vol. XLV, No. 4 (1957–1958), 74–77.

———. "Recently Discovered Paintings by Winthrop Chandler," *Art in America,* Vol. XXXVI, No. 2 (April, 1948), 81–97.

———. "Some Eighteenth-Century Connecticut Landscapes," *Art in America,* Vol. XXXVII, No. 4 (1947), 202–211.

———. "T. Chambers, Man or Myth," *Antiques,* Vol. LIII, No. 3 (March, 1948), 194–196.

———. "An Unusual Painting," *Antiques,* Vol. XLIII, No. 5 (May, 1943), 222.

———. "William Matthew Prior, the Traveling Artist, and His In-laws, the Painting Hamblens," *Antiques,* Vol. LIII, No. 1 (January, 1948), 44–48.

———. "Winthrop Chandler," *Art in America,* Vol. XXXV, No. 2 (April, 1947), 75–168.

Little, Selina F. "Phases of American Primitive Painting," *Art in America,* Vol. XXXIX, No. 1 (1951), 6–24.

Lord, Jeanette M. "Some Light on Hubard," *Antiques,* Vol. XIII (June, 1928), 485.

Lyman, Grace A. "William Matthew Prior, the Painting Garret Artist," *Antiques,* Vol. XXVI, No. 5 (November, 1934), 180.

Lyman, Lila Parrish. "William Johnston (1732–1772), a Forgotten Portrait Painter of New England," *New-York Historical Society Quarterly,* Vol. XXXIX (January, 1955), 63–78.

M

McCausland, Elizabeth. "A Selected Bibliography on American Painting and Sculpture from Colonial Times to the Present," *Magazine of Art,* Vol. XXXIX (November, 1946), 329–349.

MacFarlane, Janet R. "Hedley, Headley, or Hidley, Painter," *New York History,* Vol. XXVIII (January, 1947), 74–75.

Mason, J. Alden. "Grand Moving Diorama, a Special Feature," *Pennsylvania Archaeologist* (January, 1942), 14–16.

Maytham, Thomas. "Two Faces of New England Portrait Painting," *Museum of Fine Arts [Boston], Bulletin,* Vol. LXI, No. 323, 30–42.

Miller, Perry. "The Garden of Eden and the Deacon's Meadow," *American Heritage,* Vol. VII, No. 1 (December, 1955), 54–61.

Mitchell, Lucy B. "James Sanford Ellsworth, American Miniature Painter," *Art in America,* Vol. XLI (Autumn, 1953), 148–184.

Morman, John F. "The Painting Preacher: John Valentine Haidt," *Pennsylvania History,* Vol. XX (April, 1953), 180–186.

"Murals in Pennsylvania," *Art in America,* Vol. LIII, No. 6 [1965–1966), 62–64.

N

Nolan, J. Bennet. "A Pennsylvania Artist in Old New York," *Antiques,* Vol. XXVIII, No. 4 (October, 1935), 148–150.

———. "Pennsylvania Sunday Best," *American Heritage,* Vol. VIII, No. 3 (April, 1957), 48–51.

O

O'Doherty, Brian. "Maxim Karolik," *Art in America,* Vol. L, No. 4 (1962), 62–67.

"Old Folks of the County," *Greenfield Gazette and Courier* (June 9, 1900).

The Old Print Shop Portfolio. New York: 1941–

P

Panorama. New York: Harry Shaw Newman Gallery, 1945–1950.

Park, Lawrence. "An Account of

Joseph Badger, and a Descriptive List of His Work," *Proceedings of the Massachusetts Historical Society,* Vol. LI (December, 1917), 158–201.

——. "Joseph Badger of Boston, and His Portraits of Children," *Old-Time New England,* Vol. XIII (January, 1923), 99–109.

"A Pennsylvania Primitive Painter," *Antiques,* Vol. XXXV, No. 2 (February, 1939), 84–86.

Pleasants, Henry, Jr. "Four Late Eighteenth Century Anglo-American Landscape Painters," *Proceedings of the American Antiquarian Society,* Vol. LII (October, 1942), 187–324.

Porter, James A. "Versatile Interests of the Early Negro Artist: A Neglected Chapter of American Art History," *Art in America,* Vol. XXIV (January, 1936), 16–27.

Price, Matlack. "American Folk Art Defined," *American Collector,* Vol. IV, No. 11 (November 14, 1935), 4–6, 17.

"Primitives from America . . . The Innocent Eye," *Art in America,* Vol. XLIII, No. 3 (1955), 44, 45, 62, 63.

Purrington, Philip F. "Around the World in Eighty Rods: New Bedford's Whaling Panorama," *Antiques,* Vol. LXXX, No. 2 (August, 1961), 142–145.

R

Reynolds, Robert L. "J. O. J. Frost," *American Heritage,* Vol. XIV, No. 4 (June, 1962), 10–19.

Robinson, Frederick B. "The Eighth Wonder of Erastus Field," *American Heritage,* Vol. XIV, No. 3 (April, 1963), 12–17.

——. "Erastus Salisbury Field," *Art in America,* Vol. XXX, No. 4 (October, 1942), 244–253.

——. "A Primitive Portraitist—Augustus Fuller," *Art in America,* Vol. XXXIX, No. 2 (1951), 50–52.

Rutledge, Anna Wells. "Fact and Fancy: Portraits from the Pioneers," *Antiques,* Vol. LXXI, No. 5 (November, 1957), 446–448.

S

Sawitzky, Susan. "New Light on the Early Work of Reuben Moulthrop," *Art in America,* Vol. XLIV, No. 3 (1956), 8–11, 55.

——. "The Portraits of William Johnston, a Preliminary Checklist," *New-York Historical Society Quarterly,* Vol. XXXIX (January, 1955), 79–89.

Sawitzky, William. "Further Light on the Work of William Williams," *New-York Historical Society Quarterly Bulletin,* Vol. XXV (July, 1941), 101–112.

——. "William Williams, First Instructor of Benjamin West," *Antiques,* Vol. XXXI, No. 5 (May, 1937), 240–242.

Sawitzky, William and Susan. "Portraits by Reuben Moulthrop, a Checklist by William Sawitzky Supplemented and Edited by Susan Sawitzky," *New-York Historical Society Quarterly,* Vol. XXXIX (October, 1955), 385–404.

Shelley, Donald A. "Illuminated Birth Certificates," *New-York Historical Society Bulletin,* Vol. XXIX (April, 1945), 93–105.

——. "Illuminated Manuscripts," *Art in America,* Vol. XLII, No. 2 (1964), 139–146, 165.

Sherman, Frederic F. "American Miniatures by Minor Artists," *Antiques,* Vol. XVII, No. 5 (May, 1930), 422–425.

——. "American Miniaturists of the Early 19th Century," *Art in America,* Vol. XXIV (April, 1936), 76–83.

——. "Newly Discovered American Miniaturists," *Antiques,* Vol. VIII, No. 2 (August, 1925), 96–99.

——. "Newly Discovered American Portrait Painters," *Art in America,* Vol. XXIX (October, 1941), 234–235.

——. "Quaint Early Miniatures" and "Miniature by J. S. Ellsworth," *Art in America,* Vol. XI, No. 4 (1923), 208–209.

——. "Some Recently Discovered Early American Portrait Miniaturists," *Antiques,* Vol. XI (April, 1927), 293–296.

——. "Unrecorded Early American Painters," *Art in America,* Vol. XXII (October, 1934), 145–150; Vol. XXXI (October, 1943), 208.

——. "Unrecorded Early American Portrait Painters," *Art in America,* Vol. XXII (December, 1933), 26–31.

Smith, Helen Burr. "John Mare . . . New York Portrait Painter, with Notes on the Two William Wil-liams," *New-York Historical Society Quarterly,* Vol. XXXV (October, 1951), 355–399.

Smith, Robert C. "The Noble Savage in Paintings and Prints," *Antiques,* Vol. LXXII, No. 1 (July, 1958), 57–59.

Sniffen, Harold S., and Alexander Crosby Brown. "James and John Bard, Painters of Steamboat Portraits," *Art in America,* Vol. XXXVII, No. 2 (April, 1949), 51–78.

Snow, Barbara. "American Art at Shelburne," *Antiques,* Vol. LXXIV. No. 5 (November, 1960), 448–451.

Snow, Julia D. S. "King *versus* Ellsworth," *Antiques,* Vol. XXI, No. 3 (March, 1932), 118–121.

Spinney, Frank O. "Joseph H. Davis, New Hampshire Artist of the 1830's," *Antiques,* Vol. XLIV, No. 4 (October, 1943), 177–180.

——. "The Method of Joseph H. Davis," *Antiques,* Vol. XLVI, No. 2 (August, 1944), 73.

Spinney, Frank O. "Portrait Gallery of Provincial America," *Art in America,* Vol. XLII, No. 2 (1964), 98–105.

Starr, Nina Howell. "Signs of a Living Folk Art," *Art in America,* Vol. XLVIX, No. 2 (1961), 60–63.

Stechow, Wolfgang. "Another Signed Bradley Portrait," *Art in America,* Vol. XXXIV (January, 1946), 30–32.

T

Thomas, Ralph W. "William Johnston, Colonial Portrait Painter," *New Haven Colony Historical Society Journal,* Vol. IV (March, 1955), 4–8.

Thornbury, Opal. "The Panoramas of Marcus Mote, 1853–1854," *Art in America,* Vol. XLI, No. 1 (1953), 22–35.

Thorne, Thomas, "America's Earliest Nude?" *William and Mary Quarterly,* 3d Ser., Vol. VI, No. 11 (October, 1949), 565–568.

Tolles, Frederick B. "A Contemporary Comment on Gustavus Hesselius," *Art Quarterly,* Vol. XVII (Autumn, 1954), 271–273.

——. "The Primitive Painter as Poet," *Bulletin of Friends Historical Association,* Vol. L, No. 1 (Spring, 1961), 12–30.

"Two Panoramas," *Art in America,* Vol. L, No. 3 (1962), 20–21.

W

Webb, Electra. "Folk Art in the Shelburne Museum," *Art in America,* Vol. 43, No. 2 (May, 1955), 14–22.

"What Is American Folk Art? A Symposium," *Antiques,* Vol. LVII, No. 5 (May, 1950), 355–362.

Whiffen, Marcus. "James Gibbs and Betsy Lathrop," *Antiques,* Vol. LXVI, No. 3 (September, 1954), 212.

Willard, Charlotte. "Panoramas, the First Movies," *Art in America,* Vol. XLVII, No. 4 (1959), 64–69.

Winchester, Alice. "American Folk Art on View," *Antiques,* Vol. LXXI, No. 6 (June, 1957), 536–537.

———. "Maxim Karolik and His Collections," *Art in America,* Vol. XLV, No. 3 (1957), 34–41.

———. "A Painted Wall," *Antiques,* Vol. XLIX (May, 1946), 310–311.

———. "Paintings for the People," *Art in America,* Vol. XLII, No. 2 (1954), 96–97.

W. P. A. "American Portraits 1620–1825 Found in Massachusetts," 2 Vols., Mimeographed. Boston: Historical Records Survey, Massachusetts, 1939.

———. "American Portraits (1645–1850) Found in the State of Maine," Mimeographed preliminary report. Boston: W. P. A. Historical Records Survey, Massachusetts, 1941.

———. "American Portraits Found in New York," Manuscript. W. P. A. Historical Records Survey, Massachusetts.

———. "Catalogue of the Early American Portraits in the Pennsylvania Academy of the Fine Arts," Manuscript. Philadelphia: W. P. A. Historical Records Survey, Pennsylvania.

———. "1440 Early American Portrait Artists." New Jersey: W. P. A. Historical Records Survey, Newark, 1940.

———. "Portraits Found in Vermont." Boston: W. P. A. Historical Records Survey, Massachusetts.

———. "Preliminary Checklist of American Portraits 1620–1860 Found in New Hampshire." Boston: W. P. A. Historical Records Survey, Massachusetts, 1942.

Wright, Madeline Ball. "Search for Connecticut Valley Primitives Leads to Many a Rustic Adventure,"

Springfield Sunday Union and Republican (February 1, 1942).

CATALOGS

A

"Abby Aldrich Rockefeller Folk Art Collection Gallery Book." Williamsburg, Virginia: Abby Aldrich Rockefeller Folk Art Collection, new edition, 1963.

"American Art, Four Exhibitions," Brussels International Fair. Meriden, Connecticut: Meriden Gravure Co., 1958.

"American Primitive Painting, The Chicago Historical Society's Collection." Chicago, Illinois, 1950.

"American Provincial Paintings, from The Collection of J. Stuart Halladay and Herrel George Thomas." New York: Whitney Museum of American Art, 1942.

"American Provincial Paintings, 1790–1877, From the Collection of Edward Duff Balken." Pittsburgh, Pennsylvania: Department of Fine Arts, Carnegie Institute, 1947.

"Art in New England, New England Genre." Cambridge, Massachusetts: Fogg Art Museum, Harvard University, 1939.

"Art in Our Time." New York: The Museum of Modern Art, 1939.

B

Bayley, Frank W. "Little Known Early American Portrait Painters." Five pamphlets. Boston: Copley Gallery, 1915–1917.

Black, Mary C. "American Primitive Watercolors." Washington, D. C.: Smithsonian Institution, 1964.

[Black, Mary] "Erastus Salisbury Field 1805–1900, A special exhibition devoted to his life and work." Williamsburg, Virginia: Abby Aldrich Rockefeller Folk Art Collection, 1963.

C

Cahill, Holger. "Paintings—Folk and Popular" in "A Museum in Action." Newark: The Newark Museum, 1944.

[Campbell, William] "American Primitive Paintings From the Collection of Edgar William and Bernice Chrysler Garbisch," Parts I and II. Washington, D. C.: National Gallery of Art, 1954.

"A Catalogue of the Collection of American Paintings in The Corcoran Gallery of Art." Vol. 1, Washington, D. C.: The Corcoran Gallery of Art, 1966.

"Catalogue Containing a Correct List of All the Articles Exhibiting at the Annual Fair of the American Institute of the City of New York." New York: Managers of the Eighteenth Annual Fair, 1845, 1846, and 1847.

D

Dods, Agnes M., and Reginald French. "Erastus Salisbury Field, 1805–1900." *Connecticut Historical Society Bulletin,* Vol. XXVIII, No. 4 (October, 1963), 97–144.

Dunbar, Philip H. "Portrait Miniatures on Ivory 1750–1850." *Connecticut Historical Society Bulletin,* Vol. XXIX, No. 4 (October, 1964), 97–144.

F

Field, Erastus S. "Descriptive Catalogue of the Historical Monument of the American Republic," Amherst, Massachusetts: H. H. McCloud, 1876.

Ford, Alice [catalog by Mary Black]. "Edward Hicks 1780–1849, A Special Exhibition Devoted to His Life and Work." Williamsburg, Virginia: Abby Aldrich Rockefeller Folk Art Collection, 1960.

G

Goodrich, Lloyd. "A Century of American Landscape Painting, 1800–1900." New York: Whitney Museum of American Art, 1938.

Green, Samuel M. "Some Afterthoughts on the Moulthrop Exhibition." *Connecticut Historical Society Bulletin,* Vol. XXII, No. 2 (April, 1957), 33–45.

Grigaut, Paul L. "The French in America, 1520–1800." Detroit, Michigan: The Detroit Institute of Arts, 1951.

H

Halpert, Edith Gregor (Compiler and Editor). "American Folk Art." Williamsburg, Virginia: Colonial Williamsburg, 1940.

———. "A Catalogue of the American Folk Art Collection of Colonial Williamsburg." Williamsburg, Virginia: Colonial Williamsburg, 1947.

[Harlow, Thompson] "Joseph Steward and the Hartford Museum." *Connecticut Historical Society Bulletin,* Vol. XVIII, No. 1–2 (January–April, 1953), 2–16.

Holdridge, Barbara and Larry. "Ammi Phillips 1788–1865." *Connecticut Historical Society Bulletin,* Vol. 30, No. 4 (October, 1965), 95–145.

J

Jones, Agnes Halsey. ""Rediscovered Painters of Upstate New York, 1700–1875." Utica, New York: Munson-Williams-Proctor Institute, 1958.

——— and Louis C. Halsey. "New-Found Folk Art of the Young Republic." Cooperstown, New York: New York State Historical Association, 1960.

K

Kuh, Katharine. "Art in New York State." Buffalo, New York: Buffalo Fine Arts Academy, Albright-Knox Gallery, 1964.

L

[Little, Nina F.] "American Folk Art from the Abby Aldrich Rockefeller Folk Art Collection." Williamsburg, Virginia: Abby Aldrich Rockefeller Folk Art Collection, 1959.

Little, Nina Fletcher. "John Brewster, Jr., 1766–1854." *Connecticut Historical Society Bulletin,* Vol. XXV, No. 4 (October, 1960), 97–129.

———. "Little-Known Connecticut Artists, 1790–1810." *Connecticut Historical Society Bulletin,* Vol. XXII, No. 4 [October, 1957], 97–128.

M

McCausland, Elizabeth and Hermann Warner Williams, Jr. "American Processional." Washington, D. C.: The Corcoran Gallery of Art, 1950.

MacFarlane, Janet. "The Wendell Family Portraits." *The Art Quarterly* (Winter, 1962), 384–392.

——— and Robert G. Wheeler. "Hudson Valley Paintings 1700–1750." Albany: Albany Institute of History and Art, 1959.

N

Nelson, Vernon. "John Valentine Haidt." Williamsburg, Virginia: Abby Aldrich Rockefeller Folk Art Collection, 1966.

O

"Old Family Portraits of Kennebunk." Kennebunk, Maine: The Brick Store Museum, 1944.

P

Pleasants, J. Hall. "250 Years of Painting in Maryland." Baltimore: Baltimore Museum of Art, 1945.

R

"Richmond Portraits in an Exhibition of Makers of Richmond 1737–1860." Richmond: Valentine Museum, 1949.

Robinson, Elinor and Holger Cahill. "American Primitives." Newark, New Jersey: Newark Museum, 1930.

Robinson, Frederick B. "Somebody's Ancestors, Paintings by Primitive Artists of the Connecticut Valley." Springfield, Massachusetts: Museum of Fine Arts, 1942.

S

Sawitzky, William. "Catalogue, Descriptive and Critical, of the Paintings and Miniatures in the Historical Society of Pennsylvania." Philadelphia: Historical Society of Pennsylvania, 1942.

Sniffen, Harold S. and Alexander Crosby Brown. "James and John Bard, Painters of Steamboat Portraits." Newport News, Virginia: The Mariners Museum, 1949.

Sommer, Frank H. "Pennsylvania German Prints, Drawings, and Paintings, a Selection from the Winterthur Collection." Winterthur, Delaware: The Henry Francis du Pont Winterthur Museum, 1965.

T

Thomas, Ralph W. "Reuben Moulthrop 1763–1814." *Connecticut Historical Society Bulletin,* Vol. XXI, No. 4 (October, 1956), 97–111.

"Trois Siècles d'Art aux États-Unis," Exposition organisée en collaboration avec le Museum of Modern Art, New York. Paris: Musée du Jeu de Paume, 1938.

W

Warren, William L. "Captain Simon Fitch of Lebanon 1758–1835, Portrait Painter." *Connecticut Historical Society Bulletin,* Vol. XXVI, No. 4 (October, 1961), 97–129.

———. "A Checklist of Jennys Portraits." *Connecticut Historical Society Bulletin,* Vol. XXI, No. 4 (April, 1956), 33–64.

———. "The Jennys Portraits." *Connecticut Historical Society Bulletin,* Vol. XX, No. 4 (October, 1955), 97–128.

———. "The Pierpont Limner and Some of His Contemporaries." *Connecticut Historical Society Bulletin,* Vol. XXIII, No. 4 (October, 1958), 97–128.

Washburn, Gordon Bailey. "Old and New England: an exhibition of American painting of Colonial and Early Republican Days, together with English painting of the same time." Providence, Rhode Island: Museum of the Rhode Island School of Design, 1945.

Welsh, Peter C. and Ann Castrodale. "American Folk Art, The Art and Spirit of a People from the Eleanor and Mable Van Alstyne Collection." Washington, D. C.: Smithsonian Institution, 1965.

INDEX

All italic figures refer to page numbers on which illustrations appear.

Key to Abbreviations Used in This Index
c.—about; ff.—following (pages); fl.—flourished.